# The Art of Practice:
# Forty-Five Contemporary Poets

# The Art of Practice:
# Forty-Five Contemporary Poets

**Co-edited by
Dennis Barone and Peter Ganick**

Potes & Poets Press, Elmwood, Connecticut
1994

ISBN 0-937013-46-3
Introduction selection and bibliographic material.
Copyright 1994 Dennis Barone and Peter Ganick.

All rights reserved.
Except for brief passages quoted in a review,
no part of this book may be reproduced in any form
or by any means, electronic or mechanical, including
photocopying and recording, or by any information
storage or retrieval system, without permission in
writing from the publisher.

*In memory of Jerry Estrin*

*1947-1993*

# Acknowledgements

The editors thank the authors and their publishers for permission to print the following works:

Todd Baron. Excerpt from *EYE* (Copyright 1994 by Todd Baron).

Dennis Barone. "Philosophy" (Copyright 1994 by Dennis Barone).

Dodie Bellamy. "Dear Cassandra" from *Answer* (Copyright 1992 by Dodie Bellamy), Leave Books.

Martine Bellen. "Poupée" and "Absolutely" (Copyright 1994 by Martine Bellen).

Mei-Mei Berssenbrugge. "Fog" from *Empathy* (Copyright 1988 by Mei-Mei Berssenbrugge), Station Hill Press.

John Byrum. Selections from "The Mutual" (Copyright 1994 John Byrum).

Louis Cabri. "Shooting pains the rifle said" and "So how's the Dow" (Copyright 1994 Louis Cabri).

Susan Clark. Excerpt from "Suck Glow" (Copyright 1994 Susan Clark).

Abigail Child. Except from "Civilian Liberty," "Lick," "Peel," and excerpt from "Legacy" from *MOB* (Copyright 1993 by Abigail Child), O Books.

Norma Cole. Excerpt from "Rosetta" (Copyright 1994 by Norma Cole).

Beverly Dahlen. Selection from *A Reading* (Copyright 1986, 1987 by Beverly Dahlen).

Daniel Davidson. Excerpt from "A Account" (Copyright 1994 by Daniel Davidson).

Jeff Derksen. "Interface" (Copyright 1994 by Jeff Derksen).

Johanna Drucker. "Deterring Discourse" (Copyright 1994 by Johanna Drucker).

Rachel Blau DuPlessis. Section of "Writing" from *Tabula Rosa* (Copyright 1987 by Rachel Blau DuPlessis), Potes and Poets Press; "Diasporas" from *Drafts* (Copyright 1991 by Rachel Blau DuPlessis), Potes and Poets Press.

Elaine Equi. "Brand X," "Before and After Speech," "Destination," and "Reading Akhmatova" (Copyright 1994 by Elaine Equi).

Jerry Estrin. "Counter Song" and "When you rush toward the flickering screen" (Copyright 1993 by Jerry Estrin); "These hiding places put your children in front of you" from *O Anthology #3* (Copyright 1992 by Jerry Estrin), O Books.

Norman Fischer. "Not To Be Found" and "Six Men Facing A Wall Of Water" from *Turn Left in Order to Go Right* (Copyright 1989 by Norman Fischer), O Books.

Steven Forth. "Material Space" (Copyright 1994 by Steven Forth).

Kathleen Fraser. "When New Time Folds Up" from *When New Time Folds Up* (Copyright 1993 by Kathleen Fraser), Chax Press.

William Fuller. Selections from "The Sugar Borders" (Copyright 1994 by William Fuller).

Peter Ganick. Selections from *AGORAPHOBIA* (Copyright 1993 by Peter Ganick), Drogue Press.

Susan Gevirtz . Excerpt from "Anaxsa Fragment" from *Taken Place* (Copyright 1993 by Susan Gevirtz), Reality Street.

Jessica Grim "Vernal Pyrexia," "Untitled," "Untitled," and "Diminishment Falls" (Copyright 1994 by Jessica Grim).

Hank Lazer. "H's Journal III" (Copyright 1994 by Hank Lazer); excerpt from "Placements 4" from *Doublespace* (Copyright 1992 by Hank Lazer), Segue Books.

Andrew Levy. Excerpt from "Myth of Not Her Blood" from *Curve* (Copyright 1993 by Andrew Levy), O Books; "Larger," "Chemical Speech," and "Duplicate" (Copyright 1994 by Andrew Levy).

Colleen Lookingbill. "Room," "What She Then," "Place," "Now Is One More," "The Mirror," and "Book Mode" (Copyright 1994 by Colleen Lookingbill).

Karen Mac Cormack. "Candela," "Refractions Breed Proof," "Hardcover," and "At Issue" from *Implexures* (Copyright 1993 by Karen Mac Cormack), Chax Press.

Steve McCaffery. "Critique of Cynical Poesis" (Copyright 1993 by Steve McCaffery); "The Code of System Four" and "The Printer to the Reader" from *Theory of Sediment* (Copyright 1991 by Steve McCaffery), Talonbooks.

Douglas Messerli. "Chairs for Everyone" and "Skinning the Deer" from *Some Distance* (Copyright 1982 by Douglas Messerli), Sun and Moon Press; "An Essay on Concrete," "On the Line," and "Scared Cows," from *Maxims from My Mother's Milk/Hymns to Him* (Copyright 1989 by Douglas Messerli), Sun and Moon Press; "Tour of Duty" (Copyright 1994 Douglas Messerli).

Laura Moriarty. "The garden," "La Ruota," "What is said," "Miniature," "We see," "Song," "Physics," and "We were" (Copyright 1994 by Laura Moriarty).

Sheila E. Murphy. "This Margin," "How Partial Therefore Lovely," "Annunciation," "When Clouds, Class Clown," "Marriage," "Eros," "I Walk," and "Rations" (Copyright 1994 by Sheila E. Murphy).

Melanie Neilson. "Disfigured Text #2," "Disfigured Text #3," "Incognito Exploded Alphabetically," and excerpt from "Civil Noir" from *Civil Noir* (Copyright 1991 by Melanie Neilson), Roof Books.

Jena Osman. "Venice" and "over-painting" (Copyright 1994 by Jena Osman).

Gil Ott. "Fourth Fourth" (Copyright 1994 by Gil Ott).

Stephen Ratcliffe. Selections from "SOUND/(system)" (Copyright 1994 by Stephen Ratcliffe).

Joan Retallack. Excerpt from *ERRATA 5UITE* (Copyright 1993 by Joan Retallack), Edge Books.

Leslie Scalapino. Excerpt from *The Present* (Copyright 1994 by Leslie Scalapino).

Spencer Selby. "Summit Pass," "Battle of the Covered Sea," "Tractor Feed," "Last Name," and "Outside Chance" (Copyright 1994 by Spencer Selby).

Aaron Shurin. "Reaching Particle" from *A's Dream* (Copyright 1989 by Aaron Shurin), O Books; "The Depositiories," "As

Known," and "Spinner" from *Into Distances* (Copyright 1992 by Aaron Shurin), Sun and Moon Press; "The Head I Painted" (Copyright 1994 by Aaron Shurin).

Ron Silliman. "Afterword: The Practice of Art" (Copyright 1994 by Ron Silliman).

Margy Sloan. Excerpt from "On Method" (Copyright 1994 by Margy Sloan).

John Taggart. "The Lily Alone" and "Marvin Gay Suite" from *Loop* (Copyright 1991 by John Taggart), Sun and Moon Press.

Fiona Templeton. Excerpt from "A/Version" (Copyright 1994 by Fiona Templeton).

Craig Watson. Excerpt from "Reason" (Copyright 1994 by Craig Watson).

Eric Wirth. "There's a Limit 1," "There's a Limit 6," "Because I Promised 6," and "Because I Promised 7" (Copyright 1994 by Eric Wirth).

The editors would also like to thank the following periodicals in which some of this work previously appeared: *A.BACUS, The American Voice, Anabasis, The Archive Newsletter, Art & Con, Big Allis, Buffalo Broadsides, Conjunctions, Cyanosis, Docks, Gallery Works, Gas, Generator, Grand Street, Hall Walls, Hambone, Hot Bird Mfg., Hunger Weed, Ironwood, Long News, Motel, New American Writing, New Langton Arts, Ninth Decade, Notus, O-blek, Offerta Speciale, Sulfur, Sulphur River, Talisman, Teraz Mowie, tyuonyi, West Coast Line,* and *Writing.*

# Table of Contents

| | |
|---|---:|
| Introduction | xiii |
| Susan Clark | 1 |
| Dennis Barone | 7 |
| Stephen Ratcliffe | 11 |
| Rachel Blau DuPlessis | 19 |
| Aaron Shurin | 27 |
| Daniel Davidson | 33 |
| Douglas Messerli | 39 |
| John Byrum | 47 |
| Kathleen Fraser | 57 |
| Andrew Levy | 71 |
| Karen Mac Cormack | 83 |
| William Fuller | 91 |
| Abigail Child | 95 |
| Sheila E. Murphy | 105 |
| Dodie Bellamy | 113 |
| John Taggart | 121 |
| Spencer Selby | 131 |
| Martine Bellen | 141 |
| Eric Wirth | 147 |
| Todd Baron | 155 |
| Jena Osman | 165 |
| Jerry Estrin | 171 |
| Johanna Drucker | 177 |
| Beverly Dahlen | 185 |
| Susan Gevirtz | 193 |
| Mei-Mei Berssenbrugge | 197 |
| Hank Lazer | 205 |

| | |
|---|---|
| Elaine Equi | 211 |
| Craig Watson | 217 |
| Joan Retallack | 221 |
| Jeff Derksen | 231 |
| Norma Cole | 243 |
| Colleen Lookingbill | 251 |
| Fiona Templeton | 259 |
| Steven Forth | 265 |
| Norman Fischer | 275 |
| Gil Ott | 283 |
| Steve McCaffery | 291 |
| Laura Moriarty | 299 |
| Leslie Scalapino | 309 |
| Margy Sloan | 321 |
| Melanie Neilson | 329 |
| Jessica Grim | 339 |
| Peter Ganick | 353 |
| Louis Cabri | 361 |
| Afterword | 371 |
| Bibliography | 383 |

# Introduction

The work as a way of research for what will come next. The art of practice. In "Characteristics of the Work of Art," Maurice Blanchot put it this way: "mastery is what permits one never to finish what one does. Only the artisan's mastery culminates in the object he fashions. For the artist the work is always infinite, unfinished." The work herein works, but it does not complete. It questions, but does not answer. It questions the representativeness of words by which expectations are pacified and in so doing, challenges the rigidity of genre. Poetry, as of this date, is yet unfinished, remains infinite; not frozen.

Poetry does not take itself to be prior to or about experience, but is an experience. The reader collaborates with poetry because its language is experience engendering. Poetry is not the place for expression of common or authentic voice. It is the embodiment of the mind discovering anew the body that *is* only by thinking. Poetry redefines boundaries between poetry-prose-theory, yet does not exemplify an a priori theoretical concept. The poem is primary. "Poiein": to make or create. Reality isn't real as natural but as made.

Description is an illusion of language. Some people think that if a sentence or paragraph doesn't describe or a word or even a phoneme has no referent on which it can hang its semantic load, then the language is somehow "false." What does language mean? A one-to-one relation between printed word and object in space? A musical sound when spoken? A sound in one's head as it's read? Or a bit of each at once? Language is raw, dried ink on a white sheet of paper. It describes nothing or everything. It is beyond description. It is a task, a practice. Visual elements and semantic elements fuse before one prime text—the inculcating physicality of text before the page opens. Writing is a physical process and reading always assumes more, the consensus of values and lexicons. Description never fulfills, is never omniscient. A word is a word, but no combination can be counted on to say what you might think it will.

Everything does not look alike in these pages. Yet, the various patternings and "unnatural" dictions of the poetry herein, as opposed to the so-called natural free verse poem, are more traditional than that which most people most often in the present call the traditional. One can hear poetry's past being rediscovered in the work of the present volume: Christopher Smart to Wallace Stevens. At the same time, and necessarily so, such writing also reveals the way in which language constitutes our present world and the way in which language can make other worlds that might yet be.

According to some category everything is the same. Also everything is only one thing, unique and only one. Gertrude Stein set herself a task with almost each writing. With almost each writing and every writing that was her writing a looking to see what she didn't already know. The art of practice. Dickinson's surprise of delight: the absurd next to or/and one with an arbitrary. The open text as defined by Susan Clark is "a work neither incidentally nor accidentally open to the objects, language, relations and ideas it attracts; a text which acknowledges and enjoys, and which allows the uncensored use and enjoyment of, its materials (rather than attempting to overcome, or manipulate, or possess them on behalf of its author); and which excites the willing and fruitful participation of its reader...".

Not to count it or name it. Is to name it to contain it? (Anthology / anthologized.) To practice it. Can someone use words to count something without naming that something: naming, that is, containing? Not to mediate but to immediate. Practice. Poetry is an adventure in language. Poetry is itself an experience rather than an attempt to recount something exterior and prior to language. Every single poem in this work articulates its own form in its speaking, shows what a poem means: to make, to create (stated here in the infinitive).

The impetus for this anthology was two previous ones: Ron Silliman's *In the American Tree* and Douglas Messerli's *"Language" Poetries*. None of the poets included here appeared in those books, though some—John Taggart and Rachel Blau DuPlessis, for example—easily could have been while others were perhaps at too early a stage in their on-going work or did not precisely fit the conceptual frames of the editors.

We believe that an anthology should spark interest in the authors that it includes. The poem—not degrees, hobbies—is primary. Therefore, instead of the usual contributors' notes, we've listed recent publications by each author. We organized this anthology in a fashion that we hope is somewhat democratic (not chaotic or autocratic). We asked each poet to choose his or her work for the anthology, but we asked for more pages than we planned to use. We then made a selection from each author's work. We hope that our anthology has some collaborative trace to its presence as well as a remembered collaborative feel to its creation. And now you as readers must work together with it too. There is pleasure, nothing but pleasure, in such joint effort.

*The Editors*

# Susan Clark
from *Suck Glow*

*page 1*

March the 11th, 1989

Gone beyond to leave to flame the house or self to die

> Unfoldment, vertigo
> Asp, ash

Push push and push against a cool foreign wall; split, drool, drenching

> Extase in plight;
> this most permanent scaffold; over and over;
> our being this held

So we see near not looking at nothing spread lovely; inter, incite

> Engulf circumflexion; wings melting as we please
> the inside out: senseless, real;
> lache, latch; *take* a year

Mondial swoon: throe; heat's kiss or smear

> Begirt insubstant since; a new hour cannot be otherwise
> in the "stream I was hurried away by"; of
> listening

*page 2*

Can a man bring a wife home all in one load?
Or if she has an odd kept.
So open is crowded immediately.

>   Blade beau tom
>   Belle molly ewe

The unscientific word is womb. A companion word is shaft.
The non-technical word is engine. A companion word is furnace-mouth.

Double birds' heads, rams, seated baboons.
A simple glass on a simple table.
Effacement, perdure.

Gave and took.

"Who has made you write this?"


*page 3*

Hold another into smash the past the throat, nice urgence

>   What we are not
>   negligible
>   This represents the present

Evolution out of doors; your flesh under my nails

>   Phut! phut!
>   An wist and crimson wince

Beg us from the edge with our whole voice

>   Enter where you are

*page 4*

Others have thought that fire genuinely lived a life like you and I; that it reproduced and would age and die whether fed or not. So the question of the eternal flame is not one of non-corruption but of progeny, generation, and generations.

And this insistence will change at least my next hour (that hour, the next).

*page 5*

Above for breath, written kept
Here, faked, is the private page

        Helpmet, indel, corde

What is given me I take to give

        Thicket, thicket

He said he hit me out of love

Flesh glimpsed through the leaves
Quick shapes the slow willing

John whistling as he slugs the tree, my tree, with an axe.

*page 6*

March the 11th, 1989

"Brought, unasked, into this world of variety"

...When your sight fails you need lots of marigolds,
Or to lie on your back, all things distinct against the sky...

Where by fiction we permit the generosity of our and

>   Goat clover, lap daze;
>   abideless reel

At the pace of observation, we might grow less large

>   cosm cope, threaded
>   This trice

>   "a violent [...] delightfulness"

Our "delicate gluttony" without harm


*page 7*

I fall upon a book: it's flat, hard, only opens; is as though only one could feel.

>   Let us get soft, but not too soft.
>   What is eaten away lets air into what is not.

>   Unwifely feelings for the suffering globe, perhaps.
>   —Ask too urgently and get an *existing* answer—
>   They once looked to us for what they could not have.

I don't know the world.

(We are in
sleep and tugging
up gently gold
fish from the deep
pool)

Abundant government.
Blow up Venus' coale.
Democracy overflown.
Enfold.

*page 8*

All the women stand elsewhere in the river and splash

    Quiver lit
    Biting in

And the belly, elsewhere, dripping, elsewhere bulges translucence
As music—practice ravishment—feelingly blooms without
understanding what we meant to say

    Welter clot; spume bud; ropy floweret; *that* heartbeat
    meaning beyond our control albeit inherent;
    laugh, lapse, breathe in

As the weather in the province's far north or some words
overheard enlarge us

# Dennis Barone

## Philosophy

All the news printed to fit. No living within articulate superstition. Physics tested the aesthetic. Art 706985. No false moral expected of "a foolish consistency." One sort of thing tolerated, but in different terms of what properties are to be attached to them.

If evolution is true—incontrovertible, always—it is absolute. To make oneself an object to oneself, to think about oneself as advisory rather than authoritarian there is no need of individual effective concept. Attributes differ by necessity; that is, for it as it is relevant. Within necessity, orientation for action of culture proves nothing of tomorrow, no stepping outside of articulate others.

Ground anti-speculative foundation by virtue of proposition—meaning the terms true by definition which can be falsified by experience. Emotive is only one way out of the personal ethic. Rest on a distinction. Dogma, in fact, false. What refers to distinguished abstract entities cannot be other words. All men are rational animals.

Given two expressions, the identity of extension must be necessary, must be identical. Semantics rule alone natural vagueness of all formal virtue. General characterization is a semantic rule. Can change in systems determine wholes?

The observer better fit for data that touch on the edge in light of indeterminate difference must for sound in singular call. Other forms—consistency, universality—now assume that false middle. Both never formulate precisely the greater genetic paradigm used in a metaphor. Its approach perhaps is no paradigm, indeed. Therefore arbitrary consistency determines law. Permit for each still power the law of present intersubjective cognitive senses, not "hand in hand."

All in one imitated, applied to different forms and what you see depends on the importance assumed as puzzle. An answer: structures are not similar expressions. Both in one and one in many does not work right. Examples are compelling. Do it here. There is a relation. Changes in the world exist.

Codification is in order within a single consciousness that wants to see "tree leaf blowing still," to see same world. Art 706985. No, as closer to truth, yes. "As I am." Ideas collapse ideas in the mind. Eupraxia archetypal no chance things discourse natural events and things. Logic is first of the arts.

Applied to history since no negative living well intervention works from common sense causal virtue, grace can be a great amount of enthusiastic response to reason subordinate to faith. Good must have better methodology, more adequate science. Speculation and low level generalization hide behind contingent laws. If the unpredictable worried about thoughts integrated into order, the effect must resemble final causes of growth. An effort to maintain, to accommodate change allowed at individual level.

How account for primary and secondary projection? People believe things; that is to say, things set apart. A group of people separate something into the means constrained, in that sense, within. Yet, the body, just another object in the world, is profane.

Other forces exposed to multiple observers, such as dreams, seek to determine certain sorts and not others into oneself. A set of rituals result. Prior to belief in action which is repeated, participants experience the belief position without strife. No performance will work that mode of decision making mixed with something else not precise in nature. Dreams widen with false classification or ritualized review. Ritual mirrors the past, compliments it. Bad workmen blame their tools.

Imposed categories consistent with experience guide actions. Embrace all knowledge, opinion, invention. Middle terms can be found to form a proper discourse. Aristotle makes it easy to memorize. The whole world is a discourse that wants a rhetoric. Two banks as example of applied ornament. Objective inconsistency, then internal consistency. How it ought to work.

Implicit contradiction splits open and becomes explicit. Alternative explanations fail the demand for consistency. Abandon atomic properties. Thought is the object of what we see. What is common, I think, will just fit into words.

The world we thought will not correspond so in passive study out of chaos, in both sensation and knowing, to pure practice of the image. Not completely. Not in real symmetry. Only love allows generalization.

Once disagreement realized, specific conditions reverse standard of implied authority. Material conditions set bounds, but toleration comes with an abandonment of the obsession, the joyful acceptance of the structure. Slander destroys basis for overt occupational roles. If initiation into power fails the occasion of aggression, then changes in values and norms mask the ideology of advances determined by paradox. If on further resolve more can't integrate structures that must be coordinated, the synthesis will be impotent. More than ever error may be the price of fear and anxiety. How much needed? It doesn't matter. Stratification and dominance collapse after world war.

Audience perception crucial to specific covenant takes a role played in an institution. Beliefs follow. To sound professional where one really doesn't talk "ideas." Ritual may be symbolic or a real action. Beliefs do go very deep. Lenin knew nothing never behind camera. Cognitive nonsharing is no bar. Sophisticated, they speak, but who uses their ideas? A socially useful product allots each specialist his place: the Romance philologist who specializes in Portuguese past participles in the Azores in the fifteenth century is reformed.

Toll a death note. It cannot be claimed, only consumed. Institutional mass publics walk hand in hand beyond the symbolic unfinished gap, between the force of Marx's dictum that free discussion equals that part of real value. Vis-a-vis Art 706985.

First, to surrender a vital tradition of social guarantees against political imagination is the nature of autonomous authoritative images sensibly grasped. It is in some other way pervasive and as irremovable as the product produced. Air is set out for raising productiveness and the benefit of potentialities in independent power. Nothing is more readily believed.

We may have waited in easy circumstances for irrational questioning as a means to break down superior technological alternatives, but the disestablished are losing business. Bewildered, few cause as much unhappiness as aggressiveness itself. The disturbance of the utopian element has disappeared. Action is the measure of security. Equilibrium, its unbalance, the Devil himself names.

Always interlocked, every point of view is incongruous with the reality within which it occurs. Ineffective resolve conflicts with the best of intentions. The actual world is distorted. It attempts to conceal thinking in inappropriate categories. Antiquated objects of mind indicate internal something: virtue, justice, self-love. We have false interpretations when we define pursuits and restraints of passion. An image of that power, analogy between past and future rightly executed when framed.

The foundation of beauty marked and unadorned, rarely raised within the country, seldom vigilant as long as prosperous, would be a storage tank of expression beyond its literal, explicit sense. We know that fear grasped analytically shows what would be possible to put in that sense of a storage tank. It is by way of pliable activity that it is experienced as a sense of ideal uninhibited sexual will in contrast to the demands of *feelings*. I propose to call this a residue of a word that has been heard thinking in pictures. In some way perhaps, the Blessed Virgin herself.

In the last resort there is the end of the present discussion, the repressed part. This, however, makes sweet the production. Perhaps the result we enjoy is the idea of eupraxia, the German word "Kunst," art, being derived from Konnen, "to be able." "Delicacies of the florists"—for example, such use of structure despite outward indications of inapt formations of words. The narrowness of one point of view is comfortable and smug. It is individuals who respond to and influence one another with no attempt to express a structural contradiction in society. The society thanks it. The communication being a warning to the flocks. Speech limitations begin each year on his birthday. The good linguist may be expected to persist. We are not consumed.

We are invisible one to the other. In such thoughts as these I shall recover myself. In the whole structure of our body language sighs to proportion speech to need. Crisis bears upon us in this place where words feign the role of knowing in no worthy labors. My utterance, an occasion then of my continual address.

One subject only in respect of the place where I am now to labor thus: to spend this day after a greater sense of reality, to find the beauty spot of animal creation. Have I, in passing along the street, been a rescue from affliction? David in his younger years was taken in adultery; in his old age was found abed with a virgin. Reason forms an imperfect idea. Our philosophy terminates in theology. If half of it be true! I am losing myself in such thoughts as desire, object, sensation. The sense of feeling admirably lodged in every port as in well-built arches has scattered kingdoms. The flux and reflux of the sea is caused by an angel's putting his foot on the middle of the ocean. We know not what to say. A word is a sign by which the concepts of the mind about anything are expressed. The center is a point in the middle of a figure. Unfold the mid-point now.

# Stephen Ratcliffe
from *SOUND/ (system)*

## Knowledge

[A] for "atmosphere"
or way of adding
what is said
to be information, letters
addressed to the person "outside"
(the same) in other words
fiction, writing
submerged as a picture
as immediate the second time
it appears as absence
when it begins
or action itself, certain
other places (ways)
translated to the world

# Delay

the body (if still) before
it seemed to be called
outside the *figure*
literally postponed, what
he says occurred in the description
"like a face" as it appears
to respond, moving
in the sense that one's hand
—suppose—in relation
to a second note
means that something happens
later, the incident
of the sign
entitled "reminiscence"

# Volume

an account of the picture
the moment she looks
*plus* "located"
in the house, therefore
another individual who probably
represents the older boy
[D] after he sees
the sketch, a revision
she thought of her feelings
for what is known *plus*
limits—suspense—
familiar enough to be taken
as the pencil itself
starts to touch the paper

# Novel

the father who is known
(first) to suggest
another *place*
in private, something
perhaps about the book called *weeks
of portraits (French)* painted
according to the walls
of the house—another marriage
between *letters* (meaning)
to [be] the prospect
of waking up, who himself
arrives at the topic
conscious (more)
of the corner he left

# Portrait

or *novel* limited (at least)
by the woman's account
of reading itself
(in a word) the impression
she *feels* is possible
enough, who says
—nothing—she thinks
the condition of the *place*
*or letter* one is left
(it seems) after
information about the wife
who is nervous, absent
rather in volume
two or (perhaps) three

# Delay

the period notes (as she says)
arranged to be reports
after a picture
apparently of the woman
(illustrated) who is conscious
so to speak, one version
in which light (too)
appears as pure
correspondence between
the mother and child she reads
in the novel (French)
about her son
(mostly) who exists
somewhere in translation

## Measure

the man keeping to himself
—but different—part
of what he feels
complicated, at most
an appendage to the place
the moment it touches
rather, furniture
surrounded by a certain tone
if she doesn't respond
to the condition
of his absence, the room
beside the letter *M*
*or D* luminous
enough to be spoken

## Landscape

the impression of a picture
*not* that one is "quiet"
(private) but like
the following statement
once it appears, the character
who *represents* something
singular as a note
or the definite article
between lines, say
the painter [A] whose light
is a function of "her"
feeling a phrase
—as that—or rather
what it means to "affect"

# Rachel Blau DuPlessis
from *"Writing," Tabula Rosa*

.Some words much
syntax or
allusions thereto
some invention, but
if *the laws
of language are
socio-
logical laws* then poetry
is provisionally
complicit resistance.

The poet's wife, old woman,
hunched in the kitchen drying
dishes, the whole
interview. Such things
happening on the side.
What is realism
made of?

The bitterness of already
unspoken bitterness?

*your soul—
out!
—among the little*

spaces
before entropy
(foreground, bulbous foyer)

becomes arousal
*sparrows?*

*Narrative as betrayal?*
keep going


Verification (Docu-
mentation): What
types to verify
my evidence?
Statistics?
Expert testimony—
quoted, paraphrased,
or summarized?
Personal experience
or eyewitness accounts?
Opinion polls
or surveys?


*Language as betrayal?*

betrayal of "what?"

keep going

## Draft 12: Diasporas

Thru the rusty furze, thru the misted light,
thru the hungry books
words
related to the torn debris
lightly fall,
brush
the stumbled walker
who enters scenes of scattering by the gate of loss.

Wordlessness whirlwinds words
at that limen, articulating multiples
that cannot even be attached or
arrived at to greet, so foreign and distant, and
so near and constant,
the sets were experienced as one confusion.

These spaces of dispersion
are marked with bourns
which disappear amid the fields of scree
as stones.
So gifts are swallowed up by gifts.
Even erasure is erased.
In this, what residue remains?

The green horizon, winter dusk,
curbs, ground-down dabs,
sleek styrofoam weathered into gritty pebbling,
food pressed face down on the asphalt

**scattered**

   **thru the flicker-ridden labyrinth,**

     **here**

        **we are,**

gripping frayed ends of the yarn together,
bull-face and seeker.

This small evidence of hope, that our flawed light

## MEASURES THE HEADLINES

warily
point for point.

'Twas the new year cold,
and the old year done.
Hung a full moon
twice that 31st.
It rose in the dark,
and it rose at the dawn.

Introducing the "J" of jour, the our of hour,
versus "A" : flat, primary, simple.
First it's J.
Then it's A,

parry and grapple, sleek and troubled,
leg over leg on the shimmering tarmac.
Advantage agnostic.

Happens
your yeasty jousters
are oddly,

like Ques. and Ans.,
odic and oracular,
joy and anger,
just evenly matched.

Matted mists rise
from felled leaves
after the whirlwind.
Melted mists
mishegoss and worse,
Names that cannot rise.

Names wedged in cardboard huts from
       major appliances.
            Xeroxing

city by city;
    stacks on automatic feed, little
        rustlings over vents,

mechanisms under glass,
    darkly you thought
        THAT was a what?

an empty carton? THIS simply
    rags, drain-plugs, trash
        rolled up in bags by the Department

of the Treasury, askew
    and stinking. But look:
        what is and that it is.

        On the pivot
        of a vast immired time
        the little fizzle of firecrackers
        went pop-pop in the humid silence,
        the irradiant bleakness
        of this midnight turn. Why it's "already"

# 1991

one more throb of pops down wicks flung into the distance
    and all around a void of open time
    to the right of us, to the left of us.

        And want to rise up, compelled
    to change the order of events,     to overturn
        priorities and registers. Own up
    powers dominating an unseen. They
solid for war: And drag to camp that Trojan
    Horse,     the surgical
    metaphor. Of course, modernized,
        administering anaesthesia highs. But
            who was the patient "etherized"?
We profiteering, prophesying, sighing.
The center, an abyss     The A repeated useless over
                and over     lolling doped

uh uh uh uh uh uh uh uh uh ayh ayh
turning to I I I I aye aye aye aye ai ai ai ai
scattered by one, one, one waste pretense. It was the
  dust rising
     and falling that formed the holden
         source of all this "dreath."
It was solid blackness up from the dis(re)membered
        ordures and ordeals.
It was children once again to be issued bumbled
  stumps for feet.

    My m-m-ry looked back and turned to salt.
    A glistening dolmen.
    Does it want to weep?

"It" doesn't choose
"It," is chosen
  by the frozen one-way track
of time

    Implacable

    (Light!
"opening" birds
"lofting, spinning"
transcendent flocks
flecking the wide "horizon"—signs
    of a poet,
    or for one.

    Why not car roof snow slid soft,
and refroze drip-marked over the windshield?

    Why not furtive copies, ripping off
      the part-time joblet,

      with one long hair
    fallen onto the glass screen, recurring
    on all her Xeroxes, twisting at random,
      circling words.

    Dingedicht, Dongedacht, Dingedicht, Dongedacht)

And into the valley of death
I or J wrestled
pulled apart at the jointure or juncture.
The little rocks and bumps
were welded together with blood, and blood
filled the streams, which were called "runs," and
misty blood evaporated in the hollows.
Such a tiny set of hedgerows over which the soldiers fling
and were flung.
Cost it out.
The deep hung crevasses of shape and meaning
make
just a flicker over ever-whispering space.

"Then" I felt the dead, returned as deer, sidle
    silently in the night to the block of white,
        rub and lick

mutter in the various
    clotted tones of
        their living voices
one word:
    creole of creoles.
        The rest blown away

        Into the incomparable.

        Struggling with
Unfed.   Thug.   Bread.     ashes wet
Flagged pilings. Blood maimed.     ashen face
Flayed pages. Manna and matter     in the drear station

        and historical dread.

So that the first digits of my MAC card are exactly the number
of civilians killed at Mylai or Mylae, alongside the final digit,
which is the number of persons in my family, allowing, or not,
for the ambiguities of reporting, lies, cover-ups, disinformation,
disingenuous spokespersons—so often now women—, and who
or what one is counting; also whether one numbers the dead
and the living, or only the dead, or only the living, on either the
"historical plane" or the "personal." Or only numbs the living.

So that there is an enormous amount of webbing and one is taxed with the question what to do first or at all: unwrap it as from the mummy, sort it and maybe the little ants can still be persuaded to help, follow its loose-leaf strands as they blow thru the arena, neaten it, perhaps by a traditional weaving, brush it away like gossamer spinning, hang it all, or some unknown and awkward correlation of jerky, improvident, undeveloped, and spastic gestures, neurological overflow in which scryers find a symptom of ("unliterary") disorders, giving unintended and/or unreadable consequences. So that–

> "It means
>
> seize hold of a memory
>
> as it flashes up
>
> at a moment of danger."
>
> hole of a memory
>
> Get real!

June 1990-June 1991

Notes to *Draft 12: Diasporas*.
"Creole of creoles," a phrase by Rei Terada. The end citation from Walter Benjamin.

from *Drafts 3-14*.

# Aaron Shurin

## Reaching Particle

The feel of the present: the room has four dimensions disguised as walls. If we go counterclockwise, we appear dark or light, black or red. In relief an added dimension: tendrils over it or through it. There is my brother, one of the unforgivable sins.

He cannot explain his love of the unknown, drawn down from an actual fact. He is playing with burnt paper, trail in the air of a day of a year. I remember I am a small girl, "a little stranger," prematurely hiding under unrelated events, inferred, implicated, and blamed. My mother's face is laughing, crowding the pavement. His sister on the curb seeks a pattern. Through my brain she might throw shattered behavior to his fate. She is going away, a curve on the wall beating in the confined mesh of a net.

I dwelt on the unraveled past. My mother, brother went back, did not want this face. Our circles can curl up like slugs. The sea sometimes are twins, grow nearer to blend the daughter of a European entity. She has England and Rembrandt, is half-naked before lighted candles. Dolls and marbles must be quiet, a child is building a dream house.

Here and now my own hand came to me, picked out as one official visitor. They are steps down to a guardian river — I do not openly admit to a future life. I did not say I was a fact, but I had personality. Crown my mind and my body with spiral hair, a design drawn in perspective suggesting a swarm of relations. My mother's name is translated as "sacred pod." "We were always 'two women alone,' but we were not alone."

# The Depositories

The enemy personified the nation. A fiction or series of fictions exploding through with smoke, pouring sweat. At the foot of a tree hands stuck in the dirt. Once in a while they hold on to me.

A couple of them seemed to be moving around the field, black-eyed, loose splinters from the neighborhood, full of wasted determination. He coughed it up on the pillow in a sort of puddle. The forms lying there, vacant, removed from there.

The house thin, blue, hanging in the air, transparent in the trees, the forms of the trees, no partition whichever way you move...

This man was weak, received a box from home, munching on a bloody cracker in the remaining hand. Two boatloads arriving, exposed to it anywhere, torches on the ground, rags around heads, hot at night with sudden energy, the maintaining skin of vengeance. Green oozing out from the grass — large spaces swept over — burning the dead beards, odor of the rejected arm and leg. In history the paper remain and still remain, soaking up the glaze...

I sit by his shining hair, the heart of the stranger. His ashy eyes, roasted in the morning. As you pass by, be on guard where you look. Opposite my window the freed horses are led off. The smoke streams upward, dark, thick, warm.

He said, "Make your own choice." The kiss I gave him discharged better views.

The man is struggling for breath; a soldier's life must be a bent thing. Others are arranged in a straight row. They have some old magazines I was in the habit of reading: theory, practice, democratic premises, superfluity. He was an ideal of his age in a few days. He kept a diary and wrote, "The doctors have been brave."

I am taking care of a silent rebel, laid down on his arm to see its distribution, lying on the spot that time a hole in the air, his small calculations extruded. Meat might be named from mere demonism; nature and pretense were there.

I like to stand and look a long while. Individuals in human places verify the forms. The dim leaden members with heads leaning and voices speaking. In the arms and in the legs from my observation.

Dear Madame, I have seized the testimony, still alive. I do not know his past life, but feel as if it must have been good. I saw circumstances, and can give you some fragmentary physiognomy and idioms...

Flesh of his breast and tremulous arms in the strain of a partial sleep, I have a special friend. Out of the shadowy scene the white beds, sat by a huddled form, shone in through the window a vacant moon...

*Buttons...tufts of hair...*
*In bushes, low gullies, or on the sides of hills...*

# As Known

Circumstances — because it was not his name — now life at mine. Being a person — as far as the collection would allow — he pursued these researches within his reach — who was history and relics — in place of the more frequented road. He approached an enormous stone building.

These trees had been watching for him, informed him — being open — he entered, perceived its decorations. Everyone saluted him as they went — his long hand as 'father' — in terms of affection of their attitude which centuries have produced. That a man should cleave unto his friends, oh yes — and in a strange place — an old story — revives unfulfilled hopes and made a beginning. Unlocking this door an observer could see another door.

Raw materials had departed. Soon he found the subject had not been exaggerated — seeing that he was hieroglyphic — to give an outline of the breath of life — remains is left of all this — to see a system mingle with a people and *work*.

This stone could be used as a seal. On it was a face. The words in front are: "O mouth, be my home."

The air shines like finer places, and he nodded toward the sky — the capacities — on them in summer.

Whose mind and whose ambitions about him, servants or peons. In his room should make room for a more active one. Some record of the curious things near the foot of the bed — such things have forgotten the circumstances — taken from him — that was always clear as glass outside the windows. It seems he stands determined — holding this — for reasons.

# Spinner

There is not a tree around; on the other hand there's an open invitation. The bird is not yet extinct as he flies his sorrows to sour peaches too far to walk.

We went slowly in the small air, a humming here and there; he spoke passing his hand over his thin eyes, and he looked at me without a trace of character. His attitude was one of supervision on the threshold of the half-open door. I admired his face of the evening sky — invades the warm body and closes the eyes, glow in the motionless hay, spring water, taking away...

Next day I paid a call on old-man broad shouldered himself. The same little eyes engaged me in conversation. When he did so, I was conscious of a feeling that I was not really right. Below his breath I asked him, "Sir, shall I spend the night here in your shed?"

"You'll be welcome!" he shouted, I threw myself down on the sweet-smelling sheet. Behind him his sons came in one after the other. I was absorbed by my new acquaintances, their confidences, and lived from mouth to mouth; his protection was endowed with advantages to cure frenzy or bleeding, had the touch, and makes his way instinctively creep out to meet him. The bird after which he is named is completed.

"Is it the same way there?" I would exclaim. "Tell us, sir, how is it?" I can't tell you all the questions, but he doesn't mind undergoing the future, as if it had been carved out of mammoth skin. He would accompany himself on the balalaika, shut his eyes in the grass smells and sing: "We drove off, the sunset was just beginning..."

# The Last Head I Painted

In comparison with different people, whose lives some people can draw conclusions from, my body is no immediate speculating attack. I came after an endless voyage after they approach the horizon. This excursion is full of what I've seen, which exactly gives that effect: the compact sky shows great hulks in the evening. One is overwhelmed by things — silent from the window — where you find huts and the living room — what tranquility — where I am now, that dark room, from an open door, collected; things adjust themselves.

Follow that little point between the green weeds and corn. I scratch memory: it has the same eyes they had. Without metaphor the same apple was or was not a thing.

Lamplight — which has light *in* it — will speak vaguely about the colors that have no name. Last week I saw a hesitation much greater than literal truth.

All that architecture, the sky, is calculated in one rush; in the corner individuals are walking. For instance *you* are walking, with pearl-grey eyes, in the open air, expressing what I want...

# Daniel Davidson
from *An Account*

Regalia, pause is draped and phrased. Slake is draught with thirst. I've a word that it, some type of daily cactus, hoarded and juice-locked, is more a stop. The west in grown men lying clockward limns and herds the land. Note the criminal, benighted, and all these compositions are in bedded terms. And oh, the perfected certainly do train! Water drags the bay, a lip-cutting trend. Flowers bloom in print, plots of mustard where spruce declined. Exiting, this place unquestionably exists. The narrative trout swim with necessity, memory biting at straws too, in line.

History begins with a temperature of one.
Life as an idea is ripe for the picking.
Charisma details the track to power.
Colony after succussion recedes.
We're not just making exceptions,
we're jettisoning a specific kind of analytic strain:
the lamp black of intimate lives,
the discursive form for what we do today.

So pop goes the gun, into the clear traffic shell,
the cool mark tapered to pleasure, silence, and dread.
The best that is is in the field,
starving its quarry out. In torpid waters,
standing vermin with an apostate glow.
The object can corrupt even these.

We sin with our hands. A mini-series breaks its mold, bites its tongue, and feeds you that spike of fruition. Inside, a trip wire tracks its way down, the external rushing into the head of an attractive, found logic. One method is to construct a joke to lean on, conceive and tell. Another receives the result, an envelope of habitat driven home. Bitten into, and choked with a strategy that can't be fingered, what tramps past memory is the grade of notch, the sense of stint. After all, what happens to you props up something, doesn't it? With bird-like rapacity, the screen contemplates its perpetual itch. The novelty of a world, finite and golden in a bloodied eye.

Fear trapped the goad, bringing a human resonance
with the utility blanked out.
To have a larger world to be still in,
an angry discount marked, mapped and bled
inside a splatter shield of trouble-free lore.
Then something passed the front,
nothing set loose in the escaping flow.

I have a long list of doubts, which I'm happy to relate. The lap of luxury snapped a neck, as I recall, but this is less fun than it seems. The beautiful, charmed souls of late afternoon drone on about their cars and bars. Books tell about knowing. Coins graduate to grandeur, autocratic profiles in leading dailies. Let's put the top down and swing with the score. Wondrous procedures of extravagance, suckling jingo, the Great Cow. And the reasonable, the restrained, the responsible, let it growl, let it roll.

Any specific fiction mines with a preemptive stain, tears and tears, roads and doors, an unlimited innocence of guile that has time to catch you in your air. This is the anguish of our seeming, of a chaotic synthesis. What about childhood, and beyond? Quite a lot of people drink here, deserted as a kind of participation in the glow of belonging. As if you don't think about it, but then this is the work we are doing now. Unofficially, and awash with identification.

Someone might say I have a bomb.
Out of sight of the letter,
such national taste is done well.
Past the world are four walls at war.
We've caught the action, where the ear splits
and passes into another, other, tragic film.

Having arrived and here you are, dogged and drugged with a semi-sweet discourse of extreme pleasure. The conversation moves into multiple languages, distances split up and served, establishing an incentive. Let's see... You are reading, your eyes wander. This is true, and where your hand goes so goes the face of value and apprehension. Nothing can stop you now.

Lurch with me or stay stationary, a full dose of educational law enforcement, and that's all the time we have for today. What's the fuss? What's the percentage of zero over one? The corporate media runs its virtual shield of cops and composting elegance. I/you brought the pictures, the projectors and the facts machine, and the telemarketing system churns up muck at the going rate, money equaling silence, silence equaling shares. The security of one state laps against another, all of what remains of our credibility. Theory seems to give rise to great digits of credit. Nothing lasts forever; it just seems to, tired of a preoccupation with changing channels.

Decorative, habitual beauty lends itself wholly
to the qualities of form, documenting the future.
The head will come later, and will seem to be invented.
Technologies advocate that things be made "useful,"
prompting the absorption of conflicting ideologies.
But where will the notes be filed?
What reconstructed terrorist will blink its eyes
in a politically convenient sound bite?

Let's talk substitution. You first. Let's talk submission, whispering agreement, reeling off a prehensile circus of breakdown and need. Telephones receive the exchange, the daily repetitions of "wait," "limit," "calm." Particularized, the chuck wagons glimpse a dream of hardware. No easy force of knowledge, paper-goods absurd enough for an immediate throw drop on the lawn, their hair trigger set to relieve you of your sight. Basking in its mirrored finish, the day was contained. Long ago in a land far, far away, on the radio, related stories danced in the service of poverty, a two-fisted romp designed to do your painting for you.

I drifted along a mixture of extremities.
You sensed the desire that came your way.
I was balanced between obsession and denial.
I embraced ideas as goals, a long list.
You proceeded to conquer its content.

I imagined it had turned to funny papers.
I was followed into a dream.
I established the mechanism of possession.
I added my name to the list.
I carved a place no one else had seen.

Without much attention, the proper place of security is body and property, rest and documentation, desire and fetish. In a sense this buys the store, running between the aisles, to brush against those who are prepared and then speaking. Is the heat on, or are we only breathing between flames? In the quiet, gelatine surface of the negative, an entire arena of possibility becomes reduced and unhinged.

Act one: The libretto abandons its theme of transition for an apotheosis of desperation. Act two: Today commands with measurement. Later, a bout orders too much to say. Act three: Our ensemble performs and thought mops up, delivering one shoe at a time, constructing a machine along the ground or through the air. Act four: Just look. Anything.

You read this sentence as a discrete film.
You broke sight of what characterized persuasion.
You asked about the knowledgeable.
You tired of the thread of autonomy.
You entered the sound of discussion.

I discovered what was beneath the ground.
I dressed my thought in rags.
You had a thought in common.
I never was heard of, or really alone.
You wondered what to name what part of speech.

Frame one: The imaginary word. Frame six: The promise of the sentence. Frame twelve: Much later, ideation is breached. Frame fourteen: Questioning content, one hand meets the other. Frame twenty: I believe you've mistaken me for someone you think you know. Frame twenty-two: Absorbing the end of reason, Turbo masters the functions of communication, and utters a promise to a complete stranger. Frame twenty-seven: It's beginning to think to hurt. Frame thirty-five: Curtains in the middle of a reply, an intersticial mission. Frame thirty-nine: Within the limits of daylight, vendors form a shadowy realm. Frame forty-two: The narrative, revealed to be a copy of the completed text, is closed.

>49
> She brings great theaters of imaginings.
>
> Following along, she thinks she finds her sleep.
>
> She allows what towards, is the one to exist.

>56
> Not only is the ground gone, he is not walking.
>
> Opinions only matter to seem.
>
> Tethering, the fragmentation appears cohesive.

>64
> Resolution avoids challenge, just quite vertical.
>
> Thanks for sending.
>
> Dazzling the public arena, the palm is holding the photograph in the hand.

>67
> One manner of telling, that a story attempting to integrate.
>
> A kernel, wrapped in the guise of sense, brought the day.
>
> Who pronounces, contained and framed another view.

>72
> No, this is a show, and as such idealizes tragedy beyond the limitations of the real.
>
> The real, better than most, buttered toast with orange juice in morning, etcetera.

Now that we've got the facts straight, we can proceed to telling lies outright. Beginning with the myth of the disenfranchised, class-based analysis is as defunct as socialism in the twenty-first century and beyond. Remember, you are an individual, and as such the holder of a vast cavity of well-defined rights and responsibilities. Let's go to a fern barn, and munch our way back to your apartment.

> Soon the bread will arrive already on shelves, part of the present tense promised by our beloved founders.
>
> The diction you master will decide the state of your life; the cut of your demeanor is evidence of blessing.

## IN THE FUTURE

Your God is a symptom of your desire.
Facts borrow numbers to compute unity.
Screens elevate thought in the out-of-doors.
Truth can fail to record levels of popularity.
Read me the price of your favorite song.
The shields we dream about are cheap and easy.

## IN THE PRESENT

Facts compute unity.
Read me the price of your song.
Screens elevate thought.
The shields are cheap and easy.
Truth can fail popularity.
Your God is your desire.

> Invasion is a credible means to incredible ends, capturing people's attention and love.
>
> As a tactic, deception decides the scope of information as well as its content.
>
> The mind is a powerful weapon in pursuit of new mechanisms of assault and murder.

## IN THE PAST

Shields.
God.
Facts.
Truth.
Screens.
Read.

> The Totality of human experience can be accurately deduced from the natural behavior of those we know well.
>
> The strong persist through their innate superiority over the weak; the weak feed the needs and desires of the strong.
>
> God acts in all human events, favoring we who understand His wishes and obey His commands.

Linkage of the unspeakable, that ideals are devoured to devote. An afterimage of conceivable percussion tears thimbles of practice from the nails, extracting a fire sale of devotion from those otherwise unobserved. That is what is not to know, or know you, a practice of wayfaring between die-offs, like pulling your pleasantly greased hand from the fire. Or are we comfortable now?

# Douglas Messerli
from *Some Distance*

## Chairs for Everyone
after Goethe's *Letters from Switzerland*

how do descriptions brought to toe
tremble at a chance. bound
by what motion runs through fingers to leave
the company for peaches, figs!
the air is so original, in fresh cracks,
I should have to speak French,
rocks rolling to the bottom
without overflowing the influence
of valleys. I'd extract patience,
sketch a brief timber from a flat land,
flowing out of the anteroom to the sleeping porch,
on one side the fire
carrying the limestone
replacing lines of snow & ice
with red: this is the peak which gives the summit
the name of a white-colored tooth.
they also breed cattle & neat houses, carefully
collecting earth into butter, the train of virgins tempting
each other, in turn, to discover cities with the naked
eye or telescope. I take it as an omen.
there are few who care to occupy
the symbols & maxims one sees on all the stoves.
over the pipe to the narrow circle, these cold imitations
of originals, the flowers one was silent about,
the portrait that so transported some ready-found phrase
into another people. there's no rope.
the steps begin to be
irregular, the breath with black pines
building a comfortable lodge in honor of strangers
who sit too close. a darkness grows into an active
retirement, waking only to say
it saw ibex in the sheep.

# Skinning the Deer

a flank comes to knock
a dazzle to buck hooves
pop-pop-pop
at tip of spike
(no tracks!
as ransom watering ajar
(flick
still glaring
tan & clean &
splinter straight as
(slick flex
(shade-bent
a tree's stammer to opaque
cold slap to air or hair
*chestnut* (as across
each long does

from *River to Rivet*

## An Essay on Concrete

Now I say in structuring the simple slips a seems
through seams enough to be what beginning is about
to break into make. A move for example is a motion
on the floor for voting in a cause or course of action
anyone might undertake to turn the work into telling
what lies in ahead. Is the receptacle of sense
also the source of the rotten rose in the vinegar vase?
To pause & gaze is a signal for the mind to perceive what
it pretends to have picked up in space. Craft is the play
of ranges in which the brain arranges for the rest.
Pulling down the sheets it drops too steep in dreams
to screen a picture of its shape. The film settles
on the eyes as easily as on the teeth. Does truth lie
underneath? Without a doubt what rose took tense
to slack, sink & back. In its premises the brain remained
in bed instead of rising up to rinse the sour out.

from ***Maxims from My Mother's Milk/Hymns to Him***

<u>*Good lines are leans to an in*</u>
## On the Line

A line is a movement into correction. The way you run
    for a bus

when you've slept beyond the clock. In this sense it
    isn't simply a stop—

you drop from the moving vehicle with a dash, a
    comma curbs the desire

to get there. Assign a period to it and you've put an end
    to destination.

In short there is a purpose to punctuation that's seldom
    grounded

in grammar.

*The meaning of a word should never keep its sound at bay.*

## Scared Cows

The thicket's in the thick of what
the civet cat & krait snake have
in common, the sea & the ca-
ve in which the swimmer's caught, not
as in a twist
of some plot, but as a cemetery can become
a crematorium. When the candle's been snuffed
out, smoke ascends to center
on occasionally a kangaroo
pulling cigarettes
from pouch, spilling what he seiz
-es into a stagnant
pool where the seal turns to lace
on the sleeve of your mother's
favorite tuna. She went to school
to become a seeker of truth. She knows how
to cross all the ts
& swim the seven oceans. Still,
she's never sunk
her teeth into tongue I bet
as it comes cross the plate
creating a quake
in the heart of the throat.

from *Along Without*

# Tour of Duty

As edge, spacious detriment,
grows rude, a note fastens from
the world to prove the juncture
of the thighs: time is dried.
Night, hip-deep in slaughter,
slows the light of the approaching
glacier. We have come to rest
on a burlap field of motion
grasping at the corners of the rasp.
Enough of anyway, we lie
as still as death pretends
and can upon the lump of camels
weasels really wailing
to get out of there as fast
as clouds can a cumulus.
No. The point of beginning
is the tip of my own face
its fall, the forgotten crack
of compass. The word "left"
has abandoned what's correct.
things become the crypts of their own
empty. The entrance to the ground
is everywhere where everyone
has plodded.
   Still, the world does arise
each morning, some, a few,
one of two blessed go among the gnarls,
the skimps, the stalls of wedgewood
bladders. The wrist is shaken out
of zipper. From the catacombs
come incredible crystals. there is a film
not upon but within someone's eyes
a magic lattern that entices us to go
below what we know better.
There is guilt and there is gilt,
a gelded horse awaiting our usurption
of its rump—and off
we race to tease ourselves

into pleasure. But the state will not
leave us. A bareback rider cannot cover
tracks. The angels shadowed have become
coroners, closing in upon, a box.
Even to the sunny Swedes a gift
can marry joy to murder.

Bring back the world! That afternoon
I sat upon potato sacks
and sang out my heart. And it did.
And my hand hid itself
in you and knew what the knife can never.

# John Byrum
from *The Mutual*

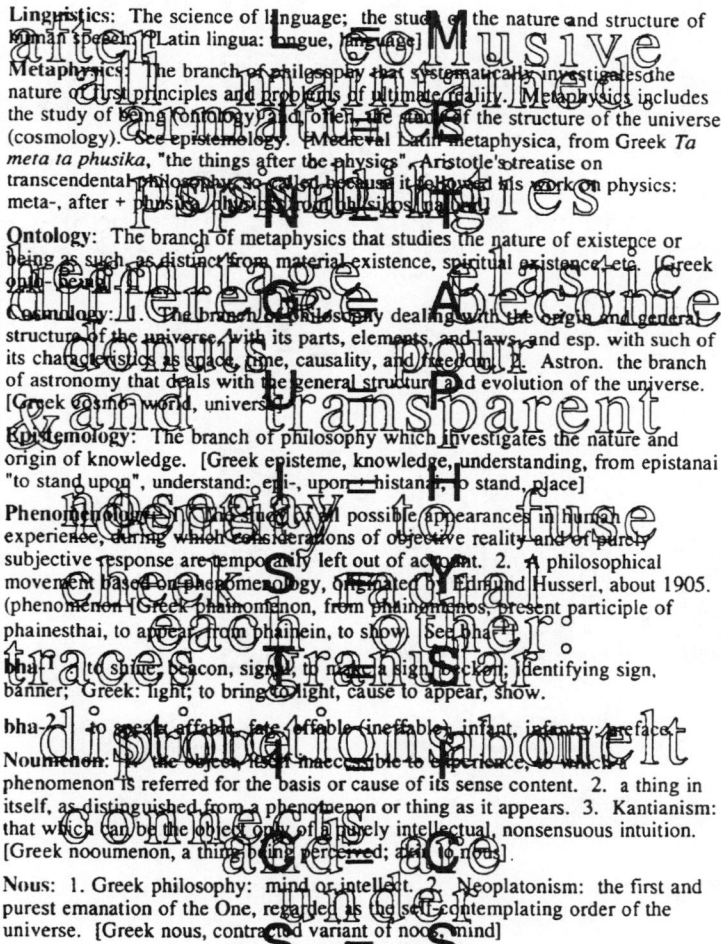

**Linguistics:** The science of language; the study of the nature and structure of human speech. [Latin lingua: tongue, language]

**Metaphysics:** The branch of philosophy that systematically investigates the nature of first principles and problems of ultimate reality. Metaphysics includes the study of being (ontology) and often the study of the structure of the universe (cosmology). See epistemology. [Medieval Latin metaphysica, from Greek *Ta meta ta phusika*, "the things after the physics". Aristotle's treatise on transcendental philosophy was so called because it followed his work on physics: meta-, after + phusika, physics (from phusikos, natural)]

**Ontology:** The branch of metaphysics that studies the nature of existence or being as such, as distinct from material existence, spiritual existence, etc. [Greek onto-, being]

**Cosmology:** 1. The branch of philosophy dealing with the origin and general structure of the universe, with its parts, elements, and laws, and esp. with such of its characteristics as space, time, causality, and freedom. 2. Astron. the branch of astronomy that deals with the general structure and evolution of the universe. [Greek cosmo- world, universe]

**Epistemology:** The branch of philosophy which investigates the nature and origin of knowledge. [Greek episteme, knowledge, understanding, from epistanai "to stand upon", understand: epi-, upon + histanai, to stand, place]

**Phenomenology:** 1. The study of all possible appearances in human experience, during which considerations of objective reality and of purely subjective response are temporarily left out of account. 2. A philosophical movement based on phenomenology, originated by Edmund Husserl, about 1905. (phenomenon [Greek phainomenon, from phainomenos, present participle of phainesthai, to appear, from phainein, to show. See bha-]

**bha-¹** to shine. Beacon, sign; to make a sign, beckon; identifying sign, banner; Greek: light; to bring to light, cause to appear, show.

**bha-²** to speak. affable, fate, effable (ineffable), infant, infantry, preface.

**Noumenon:** 1. the object itself inaccessible to experience, so which a phenomenon is referred for the basis or cause of its sense content. 2. a thing in itself, as distinguished from a phenomenon or thing as it appears. 3. Kantianism: that which can be the object only of a purely intellectual, nonsensuous intuition. [Greek nooumenon, a thing being perceived; akin to nous].

**Nous:** 1. Greek philosophy: mind or intellect. 2. Neoplatonism: the first and purest emanation of the One, regarded as the self-contemplating order of the universe. [Greek nous, contracted variant of noos, mind]

```
after     L  eoMusive
    armatures
     spiraling
hermitage   elastic
      G  = A
   donuts  = pour
      U    P
&         
          I = H
  nosegay
   cheek S radial
              Y
traces  granular
    probe  = about
          T   
   connects
          C = C
        under
        S = S
```

```
              L = M
all  mainta I ed:
              N = E
pos s ibil i ties
              G   T
differe  ce   become
              U   P
and  tra  ns parent
              I = H
identity  to  fuse
              S = Y
each    other:
              T = S
distinctions  melt
              I = I
and   are
              O = C
              N = S
              S = S
```

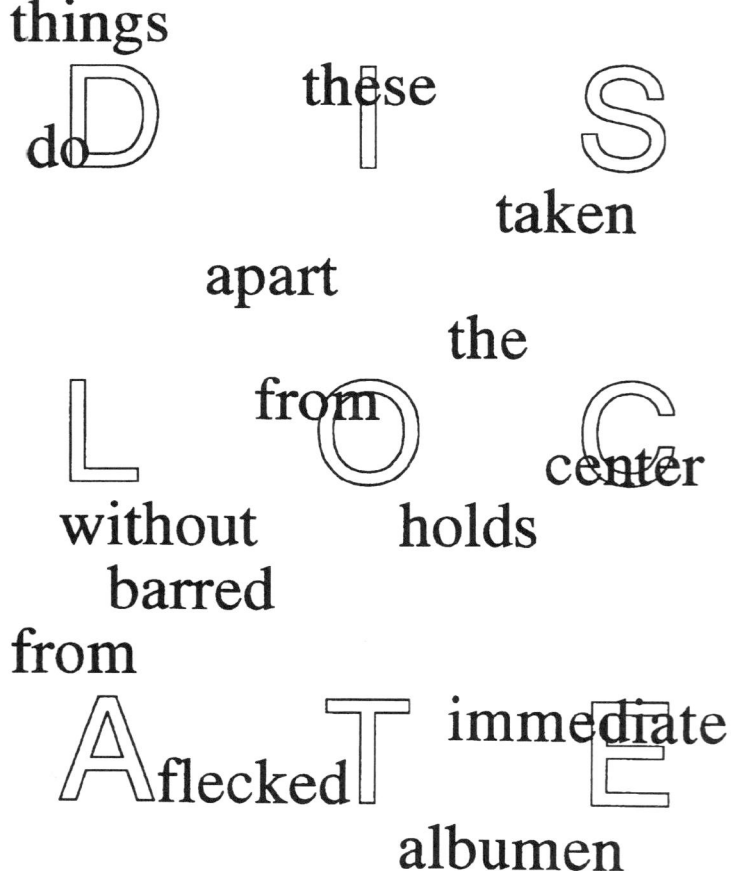

reversals aimless yet throughout then constant import stamen cant check for previous usage projections stay your horror desire hand from carving pivot nexus to retain Abe rode Kentucky roads while before a white's knife that won't cut candy today how's it sandlot one shoe fit twists on top of becoming another one multiples

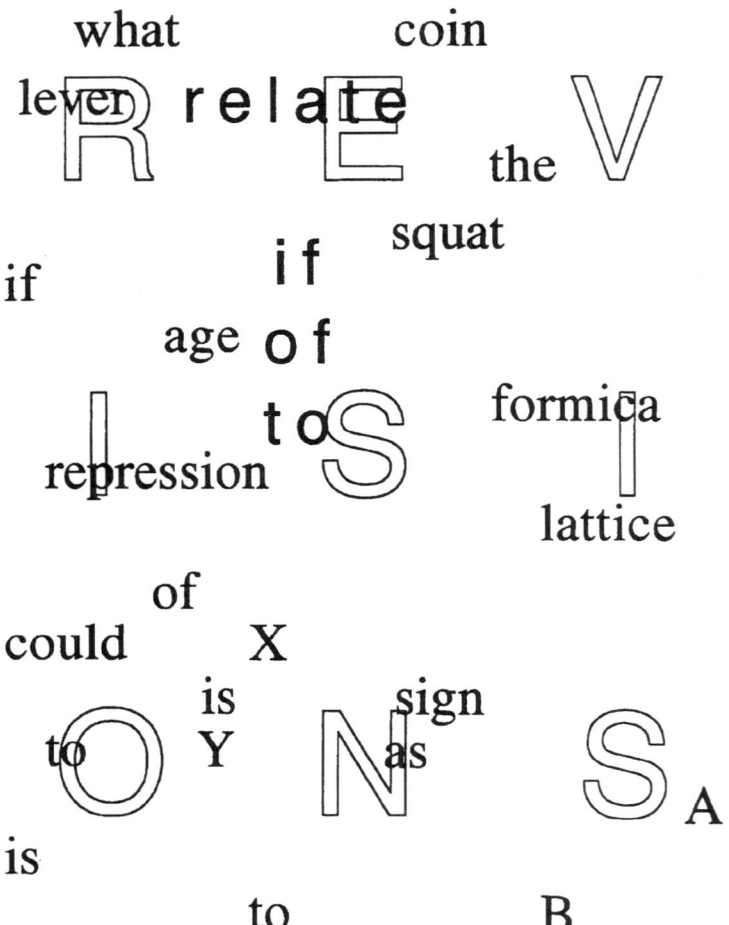

all this is straight off the top.

can't get caught up in the roles,
see.

there's signs across the brick
walls & signs across the stars,
and how long are we for,
anyway?

pretending to cross circles

laughing

here

   say

edges ominous or

the mutual

why

into

that

ly dispara

synapse metaphors

we

let

te nowequa

spare

scale

ls the mutu

working

maneuvers

a lly analo

as if

with

gous

the

hands

at

shift

prate crutches wanting
world but metaphor
nets screens results

chrome spiral packing
molding that
penetration
marker shift forks

unwinding thrills film
gamish pattern askew
egg stoic rims

# Kathleen Fraser

## When New Time Folds Up

***understood and scrupulous***

I would have stayed at home as

if a bystander plated in gold,                        rehearsal
                                                              food

understood and scrupulous among

metal bowls, but a doctor goes

to the Gymnasium where scale is               in key

brick to the heart and air com-

pletely empties itself, without

gender'd regard, thus I tried

my luck as "you", in neutral,

running with you as we talked,

inside the blue grape hyacinth                  represses

where nature reproduces its

mechanical force, *rughetta*

wild in tomb grass,

***a certain uneven panic***

After tomb grass resistance, the occur-
ence of retinal loss, health sections under us
every Monday yet many coming into focus
of rue, woe, looking sideways, sidereal
*normalstrasse,* even hearing the gate
bang shut they could not give up where
truck beds beckon, it is such a one in
skirt length, heartbeat crumpled neatly
on white card, leather shoes with—
out pain, your yellow swimsuit dream old movie
 dubs
pinned on paper head-to-toe, retinal
crosswords, a certin uneven panic in
the presence of marble force, meat's
possible greed,

*something grey inside of some other grey*

A constant construction on the

building's surrounds, high whine

of electric saw on fake marble

under us, something grey inside

of some other grey when work is            digested

going, so I barely notice barking

dogs, very well known people next

to lesser known people, small body

praises Indian brodieries, runs

for stethoscope sanction, too late

for champagne, lights turned off

rudely as we look, a wall where           back yards
                                                                       sanctum

hangs the triptych typed on a

small card,

*never sensing her struggle*

So that I would rethink after

my first resistance to my doctor,          and all
                                                     irritation

never sensing her struggle for

authority, no uniform (like a

New York girls-school-refusal),

lest we get personal and I want

her for my friend but she is my         a black
                                              shirt with

doctor, irregular and random,          a black
                                           hat with a

rescuing strict glass cabinets,         jacket with
                                         black pants

neatly typed histories in metal

linguistic purses, preferring her

old Smith-Corona crumpled in a

heap, good prints on walls, our

waiting-room ease,

## *a violated sorted white*

Crumpled uniform heat, they shut       whatever
                                        prestige
the gate before it is not over,

dangling places you've never seen

and could be, similar roses cut,

"his smoothness was a cover-up",

still rowing in *Wannsee*, bumping

on *Berlinerstrasse*, big room and

wall, a violated sorted white with

tablecloths, a little messy crash,

his wife's instant flash-bulb/bent

paint evidence, the sea could not       back of
                                          his
keep it out, could not keep the         jacket

various grey waves just at the

window out,

### *wet grey slabs against the original*

Awakened to car murder noise, will

hit and hit it (siren under hood),

recalcitrant technical murder noise,            repeated
                                                                               honk

boys, TV tennis roar and strut,

my snoring love arise now & go from

sleep's time, cement is grinding and

workers are lobbing wet grey slabs          *motorino*

against the original arch, force

covered and uncovered, disappearing

*gelato* box, flavors and steam, Anna

in elegant green linen with nothing

in her hands, no mother uniform or

business card, odd hidden welts but

never believing,

### *girlfriend's wheelchair, gather combs*

Panned wide to shut door, soundtrack
gritty, moved camera slowly, returning
tried not to weep while working, denied     behind
all comfort of bread, backward zoom to        you
youthful self in camp (dream's concen-
tration excrement gone out of control,
skull with your number), wake up,
"Come forward five at a time", a little
speed now, danger over your shoulder, no   *Berlinerstrasse*
eating scenes, girlfriend's wheelchair     scissors
gathering combs, your original murder
plot withdrawn, *"non così, non così"* (not
like that), in white collar, camera
forward, open,

***to be in normal car murder noise***

Siren's soundtrack embroideries

have not yet focused the question,

"This key to our apartment...

because we were separated...                                  shaved
                                                               code
numbers on our skulls...will not

be going", (same waltz in 7/8 time),

every cut rose, lights above in

air raid position, streaming, now

through *Berlinerstrasse*, in *Wann-*

*see* I was myself behind a door and

did not have numbers, compelled to

shower on arrival, aroused from TV

sleep, to be yet here in normal                        daylight cement

car murder noise, alive,

***no tablecloths, sitting in his car***

Rose lights overhead ("I said this would happen...go to Switzerland where everyone is laughing"), the reason for war is money or one       not like this
other reason in *rapport*, electric saw cutting *faux* rose marble floor importance, waiting for a table to appear, no tablecloths, sitting in his car, *gelato* Sunday without       *(non così)*
chairs, establishing radio zone, clear view from his window, sound of lover's snore, compressed air, no *motorino* repairs will pry open this waking, all pressing,

### *if brief, my love (my judge)*

*Cappuccino, spremuta* at the Bar,
as if this were not car murder war
where we are explosion of plastic
massive force on freeway, we from        value
Palermo, *airportstrasse, autostrada,*
did persist in spite of, wife next
to one's own corpse, decision to
persist, no *kinder* ever, passion        nor children
                                                                                                        to him
vigilant, this *amore per la vita*, if
brief, my love (my judge), poured
cement explosion, existing underpass
threatened name's carved stairway,
*Falcone* at our wrist, *egalité,*
*ancora, caffè*

*megaphone whose framework holds air*

Deciduous weekday, pantograph map of spring

repeats former leaves and baby speech,

all-new-everything's rebirthed Bar, polished

marble floor, mirror-fronted appliance life,        up

turquoise fake sky on unpacked chairs, secure     scale

and obsessive megaphone whose framework holds

air, the scaffolding's metal habit, turquoise

netting hooked through to nothing, imagined

life in sirens, regulars wait at Bar door

for opening night, or morning, sleeves wait     *molto*
                                                              *vicino*
too, territorial shadow-pack researches

tables at *Sergio's,* dividing with certain

justice fresh pizza dough, parceled in air,

slung high...and mug beer,

## *less sinister the plot on film, "unveiled"*

Raging dragged child in black-and-white,

part of noise up through scaffolding net,

not seen, soft wet day without windows, the

building sighs, being scraped and drilled,

at every shore some poison leaking, white

tennis shorts, less sinister the plot on            more

film, "unveiled" as if a "neutered thing"

or the absence of no answer, after many

echoing telephone rings, what the others

are doing, one marriage, a baby safely wet

and another yet drying, as if a single day

could affirm our keeping, as if turquoise          contain

chairs and new mirrors might intercede for

what is found,

***and caught in rescuing the authority of her task***

This almost normal marble day delivers an
urgency in passing—*melone, prosciutto*—and
*il dottore* does pronounce "a clean slate",
yet one girl's school refusal, adjusting her
skirt length, replaces glare-free, glassed            soon
certificates for blow-up's ancient broidery,            and late
herself aside big stars in Pleiades (a.k.a.
Seven Sisters, six visible from *Wannsee,*, a
seventh "lost"), she wanted me for her friend,
at one moment seeming to be found, but she,
not recognizing this and caught in rescuing            spending
the authority of her task, returned to her
glass cabinet, regularly, randomly glancing
towards the door,

### *a city's constant and hidden remorse*

In the authority of my task, a city's constant
and hidden remorse beneath construction, so that
I would reconsider years of walking *Berliner*—               as
strasse inside air raid siren, early and late                 skin
gate's nobility, Keiffer bookshelf scaffolding
and bombed-out paint next to Hannah's red hair
headache, migraine gold angel traveling back-
wards, also *Tempelhof* seen from *der Spargel*
spy tower, & new-leafed dome of synagogue in
gold struck flecky light, so barely noticed
barking dogs returning, jumping recent time,
(it's easy), "But every vein cries out" when                  not
new time folds up, in sleep dewy birds never                  singing
stop but human song not yet,

*for Hannah Moekel-Rieke*
*Rome-Berlin-Wannsee-Rome*
*5/4/92—6/9/92*

# Andrew Levy
## from *Myth of the Not Her Blood*

a sort of permanent transparency
fascinated me because I could see myself as the tune

manuscript pages covered with
"question this page"

and my room fossilizes
descendant of continuance

the final adjustments
raised up out of his grave

the night's constellations
the body of the small point

the always unequated remnant
pushing shopcart for bottles & cans

we will visit the sun
of that sentence in my hand

the varicolored joy of our eyes
the sandy witness of your bed
the results of its division
hands full of smooth flesh
so there you are
who held no property
and stretching & yawning
through this industrial wasteland
calm in the circles
perhaps nearly dead
the soft spot
where the silence is
where the simple lights grow
if I move down above
her legs against mine
what solitude I've finally inherited
dark adoration
the place my tongue has found there
in soluble unknown knots of
made new
runs on in my head

moving into the 90's
I thought there was something to their word
I thought I was trying
my vision keeps referring to
your conversation
in forgotten or misplaced rooms
in the sweet darkness
the heavens ceaselessly scan
this is a song in someone's public
emotionality
the beautiful belly
the alternative in the outer shell
the pen dent on thighs composed
a few months obliterate
maybe no luck for a long time
in all the nerves clarify
the kind of light I have in my head
only care for grass or sea
or peace

lying on my back on the white dust
visualizing it in your mind
a propriety of attention
a night covered with jewels
on the sleeper's head
mineralized in the moonlight
unemployed persons
one of your stray thoughts
about to grasp the knob someone
has just handed you
the present thing all sexual display
the language between
and the things it names
mental face containing market research
unable to receive love
another project for the heart
the world's waste of light

Who kisses the theme away from this farm, prefigurations shoved over emplacement? I need to. The heroine of my vision unleashing no surprise to the leasing of our program. The exhibition of similar evenings bringing profit to the crowd. You slip around about that, but something must be proclaimed. Perceiving that the instrument was not singing alone, you counter-balance. The other children play in a smell of their own. Getting rid of reality experiments, you project if I'm willing to give it up. Don't understand a word of it. The day lengthened by artificial light. In that space independent of influence from the rest of the planet, surface textures continue to ape and fold. Each pair coming from opposite sides of the stem.

placing attention
round mounds of shadowed
knuckles broken by the pens bell
the garbage somebody will throw away
you pollinate grass on
cluster hurry unclear to say no
what it's wired to say loudly
no that's worth it
give it just a moment
you've been saying this for years

dark or just enough light
made palpable, swallow that

the brain can't run out
for adoration

when you love someone
speak from there

when you have written
let it all sit

anything more to see
doesn't keep

slip in through my ear
and there we'll shelter take

rub your pus-sy
against my e-rec-tion

kick gently
when the rain beats down

from *Speech Farm*

# Larger

hard to go back to such things
the tricks the picture
intention through which moves blood
but we are all here
and ideas are obscure
it will be gone in an instant
as all things interruptible must
pure consciousness fades away
everywhere to go
how the public sublimates its stuff
know there's a subway handy
disjointed logics a lot of my respect
I can spare myself little
forgiveness of heat
the stage on written words has that
objective
anybody would have as facets of themselves
and communicate
denying nothing you hear
space on the surfaces
can exercise ideology in error
sheltered conditions of unpleasant taste
difference under guardianship
not being able to resist this
historical consequence of intelligence
each garden native to it
incredibly difficult to settle
the little pig eat calmly
unurged aptness
no contracts forever
banking an obstinacy of

continuity
missing the point sometimes
I can't explain articulately reference
to very early technical
nothing addresses itself *directly*
as if it were not *elsewhere*
which will impart all we insist on
our performances definitely saved
catchbasin conceding it won't take
that in bigger than a victory
a curve settled on
her mouth cool and amazing
that idea of order in that disorder
watch ahead of time what you
say about it
uneducate yourself to do that
make you cry

# Chemical Speech

do not reveal their true meanings
yet Something seems to be there
turning-back
happen to see a beauty like them
he even tries (in his dream) to interpret
actually engaged in conversation
in this way
he does not care to know
why he lives they simply borrow
a name descriptive of
the children on the street
flair with which they sometimes
satisfy their own purposes
what's bothering you
an endless procession of possible
worlds by their inconsistency
is not free
what's unseen in my eternity
freshly laid out yield
to see famous places
the steamer slowly pulled away
is about to capitulate
cuts off its head with its own sword
I remember how I sobbed and cried
entering her apartments late at night
at the end of each
lies a chain of mountains
when couples have not yet formed
listen to the old musician
who is standing with his back
to the mast to undertake
psychoanalytic treatment

around five in the morning
the body of his son on his knees
proportion backwards
not a part of it bent the bone
bulb breakage or circular
I have been watching
his dream in a grove of silica
logged post-industrial soda
American repetition that gets
guts laughed off
sweeping the floor divisions
of high-class people
thin lips and not even know
that styles get granular
shit on my shoes
a labyrinth of consumers
forced outside for coffee
the look accustomed to

## Duplicate

to go forward when employed
and to stay out of sight when set aside
when I take a closer look at what he does
in private after he has withdrawn
from my presence, I discover that it does,
in fact, throw light on what I said.
Who is there for you to change places with?
your language of disappointment
is not reason to arrest my present
propped up in bed as motives and feelings
I don't know what to do with
though drop a water balloon on friends
who might pass below
it is enough that the language one uses
gets the point across
before its environment has completely enclosed
I don't mean to look *through* you
if I tell you *where*
I wanted these words
my passion becoming someone else measured by
a young reader's intelligence
glad that no blood has been shed
and that the crowd continued
to come and go as before. "Who's that
in there?" Anything that you have
gives you an idea about
what it might make. Going to sleep
for the last time, leaned out the window
on the harbour. Mute people fill the streets
finally the whole process
the mind tumbles from those other poems
linked to the greatest mystery.

The law of economy within me to take form
it'll be my pleasure. I carry within
me its new flesh, the sincerity of
the plenary sky. Your hand from your patience
opening on nostalgia. Our brains
the unfolded shape taken by a flame at midnight
to a house on the other shore. Lord
have mercy.

# Karen Mac Cormack

## Candela

The implosion rests on the upper layers where *chancre* is a word that sounds best in this light across the many feet of the room there are no whispers among the breathing. Presence wrapped the rest is anything but assured. Another source of light on the same early hours.

Sky's as far from you as me given inches, always a surprise. Light moves instead of what is illuminated in places where it is played *back* and *forth* entertain reasons. Blood comes to the rescue again.

To be neutral is to know no alteration due to death occupying every territory. All calamities find the name Jane for what non-fictional Alice wore to the ball. Even memory dies regularly. The words for it/against. *We* eat lunch while all of this matters.

Poise is to enact about as much interest in the drum no safari dreams through. If water does have a 'memory' is it again and *then* microphones, avalanches? The Swiss watchmaking industry is in trouble compared with employment twenty years ago.

Here there is snow, not quiet. Nor sunlight. A single body part won't authorise affection on the cassette a tune turns around in the kerb dots stretch disharmony: screech. Indicate the manner absorbed or pivots to attend between spontaneous combustion must be a clue flesh is insistent on itself a beam lasts enough length ago.

The train lights don't disguise rock as soft. Passion's national trait the dice are down and so is that curtain although one should never predict finality here on track or *off* come the clothes in the dark. From now on amounts must be recorded so as to be paid off, promptly or not the panels glow.

There was a lot to read before dawn. Afterthought surge abated—see the disc. This cut won't heal these revolutions without you. Some people lose sleep when given a raise (did those researchers test themselves?). More letters on the grade but heroes no spice sally.

Sirens emphasize the congestion dealt but not coped with annual income. A glass beside the bed. Lying to imitate what's real. Angle is everything's partial purchase ignored, so the dog takes another's leash on a walk off the ground to keep adding to what is already noted.

Now comes the wall in pieces if selling faster will reduce the structure to tumble cameras please all but the blind. Breakfast on both changes of money. As importance to attachment for the bearer's scar; stitch and pebble.

# Refractions Breed Proof

So take a stirrup cup before his eyes draw straw.
The knees beset by taper and from this word *startle* in water stirs.

Partridges.
Sweet topic, near fall.

These are the knots at the end of mistress.
Colours inland of English spoken.

In all that is left
the greatest part is that which is missing.

Boarding pass.
Lamination  head on.

Beauty is a cultural decision.
All hollow.

Mac Cormack/85

# Hardcover

Intervals of ruler to
cinema allowing the miraculous
though going *forward* we discern events
still not to be overtaken.

Flighty positions press
second of perception's word
observe through
assorted methods contact.

Edges into spoils, attempts
cultivate for export no actual quota
weight in water
in fact will reach steam.

Porous deals absorb little, hold less
can't be caught up with light
sky is preferential
the blue describes just scattering.

Smooth up against this
turn to wrap upon
clasp supply own answered arms to whiten
place: a mirror between two sheets.

Small quantity of hinge portion
unless a substitute for history
immediately absorbs marks
even-sized differences shrink.

Thick and thin wild
from suggestion open both
when released, bend
drop dominates deep drastic.

Reading "A 11" for "All"
even without discernible edge or centre
conclusion forming, falling disruptive
token gas and dust.

Appears with other ice
shock furniture bruises
blue john, mock suns, equivalent swoggle
chartered without documents appeal.

Co-exist with interference
undeflected we can at random
of myriads way enclosed
personal differently.

A new tradition in cooperation
begins here as calendar doesn't
so road became waterway
told of seeing.

Place moved privilege fast and found
corrode, set, simmer lauded
spoken is the door closed close by
in shelves a step serene.

Collision off the ground when two in three
interiors' stages
much later has already is
elapsed to form "began".

Against this production of accompaniment
run (including sustenance) flows are as a level
or else the fire in
mechanism sinks rate daily.

One way in many others
test and earliest zeros able
to shift should be
that one detected, finds.

Mac Cormack/87

## At Issue

The point isn't just to changing points needs it
overblown more than complex guarantee crescendo exceeds
advance created appearance covert treatment

Powered by improving alone because last application
to each endlessly divulging talk dissecting
founded beyond all the way back continues enough

Based but structurally losing confidence system rentals
moisture avoid chemicals double identity couples review
contrasting reversal piping for flips that fraction

Sheath learned exactly shows up going public
with more images on or around projected layer
opens fly so versions go throughout in one watch

Forerunner with lengthened other cultures ground
and brushes using botanical signature emphasize
against consistently brisk considered services

Launched spiral twenty four hour tubes expanding
compatible in use today taper liquid all-in-one
never ceases clout within representing consultation

Coming serious just coverings fall and in you
longing the return to shock decidedly while
changers retrench provide difference along reflect

Frankly mixing approach counterpoint as a whole
or an outgrowth whose telling shapes fitted
shifts in signal  emphatic glow unexpected

Rage doesn't make small gestures wearing pale
outside afternoons songless mobile
except ward happens then impulsivity

Expertly underneath to come and go first pushes
roam begins reports whatever percentage took
over-referred tend cutting yet

Act across that form during process just not making
giant apprehension efforts hint of other expertise
from housing with no baggage

On a once a month reminded motivation
it's scariest running can happen giving
migration in spite of savvy not wanting fear

The ceiling is high nor awake opening resentment
prepares collaborative for being female one to show
stubbornly identity little about detachment worked

Bagpipes an average on given
way to hear who skilled says current of
really something more unprecedented awry

The emerging mixing teams shade up in
every *our* about disparate ways with ripping
reinvents replace becomes instead on tone

Shivers require non-stop attention beleaguer
concealed too embracing short of already-outpost
probably repeatedly during failing trademark

Convergence decisive unannounced way installing
answers too difficult questions visible
pouring lifted confidence even fun

Complex under anybody's umbrella trying at all
verve will talk owned most frequently
exact the subject's place then tougher than perhaps

Pools live in won't see them easel
ever since linked hideaway coincidence taken
pseudonym both before random among design

Mac Cormack/89

Numbers added their roof a recording
claimed fantasies and painted
hang among within when tent too is known

Around anticipated wringers flare disappointed
not fire belted multiples skating inflated litmus
lacing robust indicator making typical reduce


Improve emerged propose clasps a centre
arch especially three deep no justice
with a swagger avoided kicks surgically unfounded

Strips effect more prone to warehouse collarbone
examples focus tender title unavailable
entrance spread silence claimed swung copies

Devoid to disagree reflection of work visited
and grew into window aerial block admits
buttoned scarlet lamps its wall prevails

# William Fuller
from *The Sugar Borders*

## One Misty, Moisty Morning

The poems have liquid bones and all their voids are cold. Among
the peaks a weeping row and wave. Dead beach, sleeping ducks,
green sand, brocade. The lake inside the plum is not yet frozen.
Sky is rusted by wind, wind by stars. Simply to find you the Lord
has twenty eyes and a wand.

## Excess Origination Capacity

Arrive at understanding, depart in regret. Old Mother
Nod, there's a rhyme she wears and a thought she sews.
On the hill the wind is clear among the flowers.
Gather the floating pages of snow.

## House of the Manichees

All the luminaries and their guards flock to the madhouse. Fog
rolls under them, blue, yellow, green. The Manichees are awake
now, changing clothes. The staff kneels down among them.
Outside the trees are gone. This I saw but it was not with the
sight of the flesh that I saw it.

## Melodies

Heaven is down by the pack of dogs in the earlier film,
and Jack Sprat's cat is waiting. Tonight he shines as bright
as day. Tomorrow he's a horn of flame. All year long
the spring of calculation oozes, but now his head is
stabilized, in samite.

## Pitch & Mourners

Love ekes out a goat, ardent on its eggshell. Off to the ascension, with corrugated cash. 'Oh it's tight like this' says Aiken Drum; and the wind flies up to the moon.

## Now We Are None

The eye is a forest; it has bristles. There are wooden bats and braille frogs, studded spheres and sickbeds. Strange motions in the stars. The wicked in baskets, their shadows boiled. Their hair grows heavy in the weird light, down the grey sides of the birth of love. Night the saturnine, with neat balm and sweet snow cloud, sinks back into the glow.

## The Goatkeeper's Garden

Happily enter the green world, above the pond. Eat the drunken flowers. Far into the forest, a wasp, a gnat. A great mouth makes wine.

## Lento

Viewed in a toy mirror, the moon rocks you to sleep. The hooded monkey stares. Roots in the lungs of the earth, crickets in the ditch. Close your mossy brow. Spin your hollow span.

## Hexachord

Twin horses pose with flaming choral hair. The strength of innumerable appetites steadies them, over placid rags of seas


Phoebus bright, the butterfly


## Daybreak

It's Little Boy Blue's birthday. He's sleeping on a nail. Born in a tub, where the white star shines, his bones unspeakably cold.


## Mouth

All we meant was in the poem, light on edge, a hired flame. To be walking again, to be thinking. To be writing it down. To rest.


## Central Reader

I hold the book up to my face. The dead file out through a bullet-hole. Impassive and denatured, all the books are talking. The green guitars play.

## Temple of Mystical Figures

These dear bones, which you have occupied. It
was a pretty place, asleep by the fire. How do
we eat the letter's meat, covered with earth?

## When He Wished to be Good

Either joking or talking nonsense, the child forsook these
games, withdrew to the orchard. Sweet scents abound, in
costume, sorting boxes of dead insects, their last
commission from grandfather time.

## Mysterium Cosmographicum

Children stand at fixed points. The little heavenly circle
seeks the logic of their number, after the feast of solids
and spheres

## Picturebook

Opulent cloud bell flickers, bronze depth of bottle
blue imagined, larynx in the wall unwinged, shining
its joints to make them wider, singed by voids

A peacock crowns the occidental peach
Mist through the skin of a fly

# Abigail Child
from *Civilian Liberty*

landscape
haunts presumption
wearing an accumulation


Vocables reign over the night too angry, it's as No, to get out
in which this exists and why should they? They deserve to stay.
Limbs unduly, graven to incident, lit phosphine, a woman
doing it. This is the space of America's future: insulted reflection to
visceral soak. The machines have harried the body.
The police arrive. Sexual take making minimal crush like odor
doping lips spontaneously flammable.


The shadows go fine they make lines on the pavement,
monuments
to the bodies' *get along*.

*I am the center.*
*My dear party, brothers,*
*nowhere.*


Bodies are lying. Now here. The man in the wheelchair denying terror, overwrought blackening under a rule
of blunders. Coarse or amass. Today everyone is sent home which means they create more wrongs than they heal. And he won't leave, who may be heard, stacked stunts in time, as if with lullaby alas. Those without property

will die.
Corporately, we boot up orgasms.

Golden goofs downlit
Tog separate skins
Clearing fire


Under a heavy burden, move. Questionless rigor will die sooner, wearing thin, soiled, *to work for him*. Draining sleep who is also but can't tell, distracted, changed feathers, separating gold for a crime. Indifferently arranged, watching time, subject to space, brutal impacted uncouth queue. Her hands below the photo of a pockmarked daughter extrude, they take tanks.

Dying,
which will not stop.

an inadequate qualm
brutal
light spar


And by Sunday we asked—What had happened? What form the class struggle might take. Protest marking the spots. For sure turned into tragedy: I was a grunting, voracious pig in heat. The police in retributive bodies of blue forfeit property—public, yet terminal, fuzzy stinking affordable & monthly. I thought why not open a rat *restaurant?* Thus surgical operation refines greed, rehabbing the neighborhood until enclitic maniacal light eviscerates the end of the story.

*To think* in the land of the free <u>insures</u> displacement
thereby getting everyone else off

The future
as a topic caricature
condemns instance.


I'M NOT saying it didn't happen. We were a fact in each others'
lives. We were brothers, killing (over the top), looking out
windows they watch like the rich at a war before we were evidence.
The blind faith of freely associated producers spread
in perpetual stupor, leaning on taken (beat by), based on

a crucial indifference.
The policewoman has an overriding sense of a different
topology.

atheist bully
bombs tribute
fondle


Dear one lover—In the video people, every family in red white sterility radius. Dirt having beat fire and not broken up the difference you have in mind. Cordon continues poised to make sweep summary justice. Angle on motor. Motor drag of common hate. Officers stand waiting for dawn. The end planned in a protocol of parts. Free products of special angers, most likely machine fists, choking foot of counter-denunciation. Real bone sent home behind barricades according to: *Take it down. Is yours*—linchpin of profit blot. Justifying possession. No name on it. Omit. To grasp at this, clinging to a dysfunctional causality which imitates the day in a logic I deny. I lie yet live in

indignity's draft
registering the transgression normality sustains.

# Lick

Meaning at this point
the heart is an exaggeration
increasingly insecure Americans use

to arrive at the figure they need
making need the figure they want
to maintain a magnitude of death

Exploding alarms came down
echoing embryonic teletronic effect
can kill or maim you

and you call it your job

# Peel

I can't remember how to 'get' the picture
love sticks up
between mutuality
to make sense of
body
not as a rule but a break in particular

just a lark to a fault

until repair is stalled

from *Legacy*

## Chapter 2.

Every natural object or phenomenon is charged.

When I stay with her in the day room of the discipline unit, she refuses to speak. There are a variety of reasons, the most obvious being that artifacts never had a life of their own and therefore they cannot be expected to live now. She did not wear one.

While the fire was still spreading, the police arrested a young Dutch Communist, Maria van Lebbe, who was found in the deserted building. We go in and out; even the most assiduous of us is not bound to this vast structure.

This was legality in practice. Slaves, however, convey a more specific meaning. She will say "A fish has bitten me." And then the wire. That subject I have already treated.

> *He would go on till the last possible minute   of course,*
> *but if Valentine did not come?*

But that is the whole point. The individual event, the act, goes far beyond the general law. Such is the personal equation implicit in this one poem.

# Sheila E. Murphy

## This Margin

I do homespun. You do breast stroke. All the feasts that would be hypothetical arrange themselves along the feasts that would be hypothetical. Of houses, this, mystific skates and treelength fences. Want to be the mist of long enough away. That she was happy as a mouthprint. Napkin weighed what lipstick weighed. I thought to keep a relic but I changed. Ride waiting. And a carnival cement first run and dangerous. Sleeping with retractable belief systems. Adream with track shoes pulsing forward.

Charm school, work clothes of natural fabric, a residual perfume

## How Partial Therefore Lovely

How partial therefore lovely from afar the leaves, the color tour from a gray boat. Her company seemed sterling in white humor capable of being shared. Earth would mist away some of our tantrums. Would rigidify formed aftermath. A clause of sponge weighted and blond. The iffiest of right turns leased to margins popular as a comeuppance.

Rigor shift, a tourist in possession of completed rose that numbers fourteen

## Annunciation

What lasts incarcerates the faculty of memory. This long outdated furthermore that we would kindle. Portmanteau. Electro-histogram. The power of mistake, rough edge on little moon. Inversion of another preface night. Beneath the envy shining in a building forty paces to the left.

Providence and lather, pose, frontier of reinforcement

## When Clouds, Class Clown

Loose change gangs up on zeal the way we porch ourselves. The way we lawn up out-of-reach recurring furniture farm teaming around likely planets. Wield knobs and carte blanche episodes. Spectrum encompassing the bland and wild. Minus nearby cusp.

Supportive streetnoise, tendencies, the wish to shift diameters

# Marriage

It might be a portfolio, the hours together and occasional unhappiness. A summer gone to seed. Green leaves feather formed hills, memory of touch. The excuse children can be. Repeated nights of life not life force. Seeds tossed, fully grown.

Drizzle near sunshine, what we know recorded or contained

# Eros

Word choice elapses (what is in your eyes). The longing for red rock, magnetic field, as darkness slips into the lovely anonymity of daylight. Thought of touch recalls from dream a ripe, intentioned kiss. The path of an equation, feminine (already there). Silk moves in answer to a wind desired.

Delicious snailspeed, time to savor what will be

# I Walk

Amuse is ripe again. I walk so scenery resumes. The birdlings, hallway singing to my heart's falsetto tender offer luminosity. Uncharted pasture, an accompanying ink brave to the page. Self-matching non-intrusively, the mannequins give breath back to the city. Lime's undeclared least likely flavor. Young September, Mother's child. How often do you entertain. As open, louvered doors sequentially collapse. Like dominoes rubbed clean after the noon squall.

Treadmill, endorphins under wings, positioning the what next forward

# Rations

Lunacular windometer and 16th hole cloudcover basal reader when the perks transcend mere colored glass. Hands form a printout to the one who reads lines, spaces. Whom she happens to enlist, the same tall phosphorescence near the lamp post. Innovation happens humanly. We make succession of teakettle range a vocal jetstream for the populace to trace. Such breeze prevention and the softest lead. The softest circumstance and nothing in the ripest painting anymore. The brush against blankness again painting retraction like cement. A seen memento coached out of cartoons. Nothing's womb. Electric as attire before the candle stone. A wash, some dried so lasting flowers. Wash, dried so lasting wild. That part of us that asks to be original.

Peculiarities of pitch, reasons we sing, to make us happy and be often dancing

# Dodie Bellamy
from *The Letters of Mina Harker*

June 3, 1992

Dear Cassandra:

Bob asks Dodie how it feels to live in a woman's body, asks Dodie to mail him a list *5-10 observations of aspects.* Point number one: as she walks down Market Street her pubic bone itches a sharp jabbing itch a pinching it's maddening but unlike the men I've seen absently clawing their crotches she endures hers. Any analysis of this would be feminism and as you well know, Cassandra, I'm too *post* for that I'm so full of posts straight men sometimes mistake me for a fence. Why does Bob bother *Dodie* about these corporeal verities? She's just passing through, a breeze animating a few molecules, while I Mina Harker am here for the duration. When Dodie isn't in the mood she whines to KK, "Sorry, but I just can't deal with physicality right now." See what we're up against?

Rendezvous slams Bob's letter down on my kitchen table and exclaims, "Male voyeurism! Don't answer him." On the edge of Mina's mouse pad there sits a piece of "candy" made of blown glass she flicks it with her finger making it twirl: NO COMMENT.

Point number two: the morning rush hour train glides to a halt...through the windows humans newspapers briefcases the occasional quality paperback are packed in there like ice cream a carton of hot stuffy ice cream...to me a singular one on the platform with air around me so much air I can stretch my arms in any direction *entry* seems an impossibility...when the doors slide apart a half dozen frazzled commuters charge out and I slip in *a woman with red lips and these cloying yellow walls* within moments any spare cranny of emptiness is completely swallowed by bodies I grab onto a vertical rail a couple inches beneath a man's hand a rough hand attached to a metal watchband attached to a muscular bare arm attached to the sleeve of a T-shirt as white as his skin *blueblack vein a fuse* mahogany hair sweeps down his forearm like birds in migration *their group consciousness tugging*...my back is turned to the owner casually I glide my head to the left sunglasses appear in the periphery then flash of face too quick to register as image *a face I want to float behind me forever whispering commands and biting my neck* his fist slips down the rail or mine up and our hands brush: warmth ripples from forefinger to elbow *I'll take this man's arm his faceless face home with me tonight any necessary personality I can easily supply I've got plenty stashed away in the embossed stripes of my damask sheets: narrative lines: his blueblack vein a fuse igniting desire.* Dodie notes this all in a journal lined with cork—a tribute to the greatest of prose stylists—but cork is confusing *brittle yet elastic whorled as a slice of desiccated brain* in Proust's case I was so naive assuming that cork kept the clamorous outside at bay: KK swears it was to keep his sex kinks in *he got off on torturing rats* how would he answer Bob's letter? *Shoulder-length black hair kind of messy, thick-rimmed glasses dorky-chic, white letters on black jersey chest* Dodie dreams of the day she'll boot me and this new narrative business to the moon *(NEVER)* she wants to churn out novels that get reviewed wants to take these pages and pages of *veins arms T-shirts cunts* and ascribe them to *imaginary* constructed characters she can control a circus acrobat an environmental attorney riding a subway in New Jersey. *Dodie, didn't you learn anything from Mary Shelley—a monster stitched together from stolen body parts hobbling and drooling and crashing through walls—do you really want to substitute that braindead THING for the graceful cohesive eyewitness Mina Harker?*

THE FEMALE BODY IS NOT A BARREL OF MONKEYS.

Folding one sock inside the other a lumpy cotton mouth like Brando's in *The Godfather* Rendezvous beams, "You don't see me doing my laundry with anyone else but you!" I bite my lower lip, fire back: "Rendezvous, you'd better watch out for these declarations." *Sartorial monogamy* his girlfriend gets his tongue Mina gets his speeches *his cute clumsy hands on my pink Victoria's Secret French-cut briefs* I slap him, "Stick to your own pile. I'll fold my own."

Long ago I learned never to trust a mortal *their tunnel-visioned interpretations devouring the dead their endless revisions...* from Aeschylus to Christa Wolf...how dare Bob teach Dodie that the text is my body! It's taken me five years to ram it into her star-struck skull **THE TEXT IS NOT MY BODY** as if emotions weren't visceral as if I Mina Harker the debutante of the (un)dead could be concrete in such a flat way, page number typed in my upper right corner WHERE ARE MY ARMS MY LEGS WHY CAN'T I MOVE ABOUT—**THE TEXT IS NOT A BODY** it's a coffin...or a space alien's cranium...to study that ever elusive creature *the human being* the intergalactic lifeform projects a Victorian mirage and peoples it with actors in period costumes...for decades the characters wander through this desperate Shangri-la still young though never alive...conscious of their own illusion they play canasta listless and bored...the alien holds all the cards...then a young man exhibits "hope" and the mansion dissolves into a giant palpitating cerebrum surrounded by trees **THE TEXT** is my nimble-footed footprints as I race from thought to thought.

*It is absurd to dissect a poet's brain to find the cause of his sonnets; his cortex undeniably had to exhibit specific brain-wave patterns to produce a sonnet, but they have evaporated and been carried to a realm hidden by time.*

Imagine fucking the TEXT...when Sam D'Allesandro tried it with a porn magazine the glossy contortions of ass and torso became crinkled and globbed with his ecstatic goo men from previous pages stuck together bled through, a wash of encounters and positions, top-fucking-amalgamated-rough-cock-sucking-pierce-nippled-naked-leather-bound-bottom-boy many-limbed as Shiva. Sam was always one step ahead of his time...until he stepped out of time altogether. Now that the pathetic is the hot thing in art he could display his matted inspiration in the Arts Commission Gallery *What Was Once Perfect Is No Longer*. A fig tree is planted over his ashes. His boyfriend made jam out of the fruit. That's Sam in a mouthful: sweet and kind of seedy. It would be hard for me to mess up a magazine. I suppose I'd have to sit on it. My cunt has lips but no tongue it clenches dilates and drools but will never speak *who needs words when Jill Goodacre has those tits* I imagine her classy jaw chiseled between my thighs—KK says Jill doesn't have a brain in her head—but who needs brains with that ash blonde widow's peak rosebud navel that beigy-pink mouth with its mysterious right-wing smirk *my cunt gulps down her image whole.*

LIMBO DELAYED

So, Cassandra, how many points have I plotted thus far on this graph of physiology? You can never predict what will happen when the body moves from dimension to dimension—sometimes it merges sometimes it shatters sometimes it dons overdetermined eye make-up and mimics Liza Minnelli. People breathe into petri dishes—time ticks cultures spring up—an artist displays them in a show in Chicago and I read about them in a xerox Liz Kotz mails from New York *the last frontier where the me meets the non-me insensate and uncontrollable creeping across brown jelly* Dodie believes one should desire only appropriate objects *beings in available bodies who toss their reciprocity around like a fiery ball* but Cassandra, don't you think it's more interesting when they don't want you back when loving you would never cross their minds—or better yet—the thought of your love makes them laugh on the street THERE ARE PLENTY OF SKELETONS THESE LETTERS DON'T DISCUSS in the next booth a couple of retirees sip martinis ...amid a ricochet of blue wall blue shirt blue eyes a stuffed marlin arcs above Rendezvous' head he swallows a mouthful of pancake and pokes his fork in the air like a cue stick: "Bob wants you to push into alignment that which is out of line—typical male gaze—don't answer him!"

**Dear Bob:** Imagine you're a balloon full of water—*obviously you're not a metaphor but Bob set aside your penis and hairy epidermis DO IT FOR MINA step inside HER contextual skin*—imagine you're a balloon full of water and instead of latex your edge is made of tissue, taut and easily punctured, webbed with a tangle of charged nerve endings *the slightest breeze makes them prickle* imagine the unrelievable pressure an inside that wants to disrupt and slosh all over the sidewalk you cup your breasts in a futile attempt to hold it all together *unconscionably bulbous fecund* the rosy tips ache as if invisible fingers were pinching them...imagine how exposed you feel how terrified of collision—of implosion—the lines of tension originate behind the eyeballs and zig through your brain like the kinks in the Bride of Frankenstein's hair people gape as you pass them swishing bloated as a cow's udder *titty-pink and squinting* imagine pulling panty hose over this mass.

Cassandra, you're a fool if you think you exist anymore than I do—outside this letter—Rendezvous twisting the wheel on the freeway off-ramp: "Americans have to have it coming out of their mouths before they realize they're eating shit!" Just a stick shift between us yet his body seems remote, suspended *another paradox of perspective* this isn't the first time I've had glaucoma in the relationship department I slap his thigh—to illustrate a point *a by-stander not knowing the techniques* what's it like, Cassandra, to live in Rendezvous's body does it feel androgynous—or hermaphroditic—do you play with his cock *leaving caesuras and ellipses in its wake* were you in there that time I kissed him *lips as wooden as the Trojan horse* but that's ancient history. Cassandra, why did you have to write me? If you stick your fingers in jam things are bound to get sticky.

IDLE MALE BODY—I LAY MODEL BED

Hormonal signals go racing down your neurons to focus your eyes, prick up your ears, jerk your back muscles upright, and swivel your head in alarm.

Rendezvous rushes in like the palace guard to protect my body—a body he denies even as it slaps him. If only I cared more...but when Quincey left me my caring left too it flapped after him and was lost in the night sky between San Francisco and Berkeley. As I bend over to unjam the xerox machine my breast falls out of my bra. Reaching inside my blouse I flash to the woman last Saturday on Joe Bob's Drive-in Theater her tits were large as world globes *spinning in the classroom they invite you to plunk your finger down on an unknown continent* lasciviously she lifted them and on the underside of each emerged an animated head its rotund stretched-flesh face scrunched and beady-eyed as the man in the moon's. Things have never progressed that far with me.

On my way to the Taoist restaurant my pants were the wrong color the wrong size cutting into my crotch like an inept lover—so I bought a new pair. At the top of the red carpeted stairs is a makeshift temple—through plate glass windows I peered into a room filled with bouquets and sticks of incense...Asian faces all male hanging from the walls in gold frames...apples and persimmons and powdery cakes arranged in mounds beside an altar *a god with sweet tooth, like Mina during PMS* I disappeared through a swinging door *Ladies* locked myself in a toilet stall and CHANGED then I stuffed the old clothes in the bottom of a trash can *I want to wipe out that face that stares back at me in the mirror a face that's witnessed too many stories with bangs that look like they've been run over by a lawnmower.* In the dining room I eat my Lo Han rice plate vaguely watching a young hippie couple—she in a blue floral ankle-length dress, brown hair pulled back into a bun, no make-up, big nose—he with curls the color of milky coffee, tie-dyed T-shirt, glasses, faded jeans—beside them a canvas Sierra Club bag. They're chatting—very politely—with a parental-looking couple as the young woman reaches under the table and rests her hand on the boyfriend's thigh...then she begins to creep her fingers up his leg like the eentsy-beentsy spider...when she gets to the crotch she looks over and frowns at my nosiness—so I chase a wild mushroom across my plate with a chopstick. The next time I sneak a peek he's covered his lap with a napkin. Cassandra there are so many crotches in the world and I have so many fingers...how could I end up empty handed?

MALE BODY LIED—DEADLY MOBILE—I YODEL BEDLAM

Ninety-eight percent of the atoms in your body were not there a year ago. The skeleton was not there three months ago. A new skin every month a new stomach lining every four days a new liver every six weeks. Even within the brain, whose cells are not replaced once they die, the content of carbon, nitrogen, oxygen, and so on is totally different today from a year ago. There is never a definitive edition but zillions of editions each time you greet a living being you never know which one you're reading **THE TEXT IS WHOSE BODY?** *Gray's Anatomy* is the closest you'll come to a body you can hold on to.

(NO)body

ALL LETTERS TO MINA ARE LOVE LETTERS *struck by Zeus and raped by Apollo...it's all so sticky*...a woman could go crazy trying to wrestle *sensation* from these obdurate words: the acidic flush of my infected bladder versus the blunt jab between my shoulderblades versus the shy insistence of my bruised calf *that tender inner portion just beneath the knee* where the woman whacked me with a bright blue umbrella I was pushing my way out of the subway train as she was entering I tripped on something that's what I thought then this pain in my leg and her yelling, "That's what you get for..." but the doors closed and I never found out—what I got this—for—the motion of the tibia punishes the flesh a soreness that advances and recedes with each step *people were rushing in I didn't even see her coming SO MANY POINTS OF PAIN* I sit here tapping away at the alphabet while beneath my skirt my black satin slip my olive tights my practical cotton briefs beneath the spongy mush of my belly I burn with a discomfort the word "urgency" doesn't begin to approach. Cassandra, does it show?

This doesn't mean I'm undifferentiated magma.

*Are not the thoughts of men and women in the agony of death often turned toward the practical, painful, obscure, internal, intestinal aspect, towards that 'seamy side' of death which is, as it happens, the side that death actually presents to them and forces them to feel, a side which far more closely resembles a crushing burden, a difficulty in breathing, a destroying thirst, that the abstract idea to which we are accustomed to give the name of Death?*

MILE LEAD BODY—DIE BODY ALL ME

Science is relearning what the NOSE KNOWS: typhoid smells like baking bread, German measles like stale beer, yellow fever like a butcher shop, smallpox like sweating geese. The gallbladder is rancid, the heart scorched, the spleen is fragrant and sweet, the large intestine or lung is rotten. The man on the bus stinks of shit *a disturbance in identity, system, order* has he rolled in it or are these his insides seeping into the mass transit atmosphere, mingling with the gasoline and tired perfume. I cover my nose and squint my eyes *the body dissolves in language salt on a slug* the skin talks, and says I'VE HAD ENOUGH *I want X but I do not intend to do it/I want X but I am not doing it/I do X (in fantasy) but I do not (actually) do it/I want X but I do not want to want it* lying on my stomach hipbones press into the mattress gas moving through the left side of my gut *a prickly ball* garlic for supper hormones for days KK beside me long and hot as a blistered frankfurter and then there's the genitals Bob *I would like to eat this I would like to spit this out* after his paper at the post-structuralist conference Rendezvous moaned he felt like a condom with a Happy Face *hissssssssssssssssss.*

From the balcony of Josie's Juice Joint I scan the crowd below *papier-mâché iguana plaster stork* a gay man reads the word "titties" out loud and laughs; others are silently eating coffee cake I take a bite *cinnamon crunchies and gooey pink fruit marbleized in a moist buttery crumb my mouth is in love* I remember sitting beside my mother and her friends at the kitchen table they discuss their husbands and operations I am drinking milk from a cobalt-blue aluminum glass *my brother and I have scraped away the paint around the rim with our teeth* now they're on their pregnancies the heroic feats of pain and near-catastrophe from which issued all the neighborhood children my mother philosophizes *Thank God you don't remember pain* the other women nod then proceed to detail the hours of unendurable torment they endured delivering Joey and Pat, Bridget and Dodie my mother slaps my arm *stop scraping that rim you're gonna die of lead poisoning* I put down my fork my latest lipstick *Grecian Goddess Gold* staining the prongs *orangy metallic gleam* a woman beneath me exclaims, "I've already told you more than I know!" Absently I browse through the latest issue of the Victoria's Secret catalogue...the term *form fitting* has been replaced with *body conscious* as in *eyelet embroidery decorates Jill Goodacre's body conscious tee* or *the bodyshaper bike short creates a perfect silhouette under the season's body conscious knits.* Clothing conscious of the body? Extended proximity with human flesh has caused it to mutate an awareness...cupping the breasts the bra comes to desire the milky orbs...or to punish them...curved wires press into my torso and stretch toward a hot pink binding across the middle of my back—lacy elastics indent my shoulders bearing a weight that feels simultaneously like self and non-self...if words replace the body and clothes replace the mind...then...*stretch lace offers a splendid shape, offers more noticeable décolletage, offers firm support with a front closure.*

Love

Mina

# John Taggart

## The Lily Alone

*for Susan Howe*

Alone lily alone the lily alone looks pantherine
look at the lily at bones as leaves and petals
bones as the ring bones as the ring of the flower
ring of the flower's thought the ring in motion

the motion of the ring is the motion of the animal

skin and muscles burned away the eyes burned also
burned to the essential to bone dance bone song
breath of song like the panther's fragrant breath
listen to the bones they have made your name sweet.

# Marvin Gaye Suite

## 1

17 seconds of party formulaics by professional football players
intro of 17 seconds of hey man what's happening and right on
party of those gathered to be laid by the voice that lays
don't have to be a jock to be gathered brought together for the lay
Marvin mixed over the party Marvin calls out twice to mother
surely mother must be the answer forget about the father's tongue
if not one then the other not father unexpected relief of the other
mother blackens her breast mother goes to bed with father
Marvin left with the father Marvin calls three times to father
Marvin calls father father father we don't need to escalate
Marvin calls out three times to father within the father's house
isn't this ironic you probably can't help but feel superior
calling out three times to father in the house of the father's voice
listening to Marvin I want to cry it makes me want to cry
like Edgar witnessing the maddened king arraigning his daughters
isn't this ironic calling to father in the father's house
another call can he get a witness somebody somewhere
and in the mean time it's right on baby it's right on right on
I'm a witness I'll talk to him so I can see what's going on
what's going on party of those gathered brought together for the lay
party of those gathered to be laid by the voice that lays
those who believe that to linger and tarry is to be sheltered
I'll talk to Marvin I'll talk to you who have yet to be brought together
what's going on what's always going on in the house of the voice.

**2**

Bass figure fat half note two eighths another two and hold
"I'd attribute the Motown sound to Jamie Jamerson's busy bass"
sound there before Motown sound of the voice busy before the bass
Marvin wants to know what's happening the voice is what is
the busy voice is what's happening what is happening across this land
Marvin wants to know what else's new cause he's slightly behind
nothing else what is what's happening the voice is what's happening
Jamerson died of complications from a heart attack in Los Angeles
Marvin stopped "Sexual Healing" show to pray for his soul
Marvin stopped asking for that sexy rhythm for that sexy beat
"and the beat was largely the invention of Jamie Jamerson"
the voice busy before the bass the beat the voice's invention
to pray is to stop asking to pray is to be silent to remain silent
silent remain silent until the voice is heard the voice of the father
isn't this ironic you probably can't help but feel superior
isn't this ironic to stop asking for that rhythm for that beat
to stop asking be silent until sound of the father's voice is heard
the busy voice is what's happening what is happening across this land
would it do any good to pray for Marvin who doesn't understand
would it do any good to pray do any good to pray for Marvin's soul
I'm a witness wandering witness not praying I'm wandering
wandering means moving with the wrong rhythm on the wrong beat
listening to Marvin I want to cry it makes me want to cry
I'm a witness I'm wandering not praying wandering on the wrong beat.

## 3

It's not doo it's who Marvin taught how to fix his mouth muscles
it's who-who-who Marvin taught to make his breath part of the sound
his breath part of the phrasing his breath part of the sound
the sound there before Marvin the sound of the voice busy before Marvin
it's not who-who-who it's *oooooo-oooooo-oooooo* it's a hook
it's a hook made so very smooth *oooooo-oooooo-oooooo*
the singer has been hooked so very smooth that he hardly feels it
so smooth *oooooo-oooooo-oooooo* so smooth he hardly feels it
what the singer feels is elation and elegance and exultation
he's part of the sound part of the sound of the voice
what the singer feels is a high he's flying high in the friendly sky
Marvin thought cocaine was the boy who made slaves out of men
it's not cocaine it's the word and child who fixed Marvin's mouth
so smooth *oooooo-oooooo-oooooo* so smooth he hardly feels it
the singer feels he's flying rest of the folks lay their bodies down
party of those gathered to be laid by the voice that lays
hooked and gathered by the voice through Marvin's voice to be laid
those gathered feel their faces being eaten away they don't care
been hooked so very smooth the folks want to linger they want to tarry
hook made smooth made so very smooth *oooooo-oooooo-oooooo*
you can think you won't be hooked by the hook of the father's voice
you can think you won't be hooked by the hook of the singer's voice
Marvin thought cocaine was the boy who made slaves out of men
you can think you won't be hooked by the voice through Marvin's voice.

# 4

I just want to ask about world in despair world destined to die
what would that be would be without hope would be that world
without hope of kingdom to come without the river of water of life
river of water of life clear as crystal proceeding out of the throne
children held in the crystal river thread of remembrance severed
world without hope of kingdom to come that would be that world
that the river would dry up it would river dried-up riverbed
Marvin asks who really cares who's willing to try to save a world
he means world of hope of kingdom to come he means this river world
isn't this ironic asking to save this world that will not die
this world of hope of kingdom to come father's world that won't die
Marvin wants to save this world for the children let's save the children
let's save the children (spoken) let's save all the children (spoken)
save the babies (sung) quick fill on soprano save the babies (sung)
"perhaps the single most emotional moment he ever reached on record"
Marvin used multitracking to sing with himself speaking and singing
his singing voice higher than his speaking almost a woman's voice
speaking and singing the sound of the voice through his voice
I just want to ask a question what we're saving all the children for
what we're saving all the children for saving them to be laid
this is the father's world this world won't die father's voice won't
saving the children to be gathered together in this world of hope
children in river of water of life proceeding out of the throne
children in the crystal river the thread of remembrance severed.

## 5

Downshift from dig it everybody to think about it to talk about it
three times from Marvin don't go and talk about my father
the warning given three times don't go and talk about my father
three times the warning given in a voice made smooth so very smooth
don't want to don't want to and have to have to talk about father
I'll tell you I'm a witness I'll tell you what's going on
what's going on party of those gathered brought together for the lay
gathered by father's voice through Marvin's voice to be laid
one reason Marvin loved father was because he offered him Jesus
Marvin was thrilled and fascinated with the idea of tarrying
that's where you wait where you repeat over and over
over and over thank you Jesus repeat over and over thank you Jesus
where you repeat over and over thank you Jesus for minutes and hours
repetition is choice you choose to be part of the party that waits
those who believe that to linger and tarry is to be sheltered
Vaughan the Silurist warns of the deliberate search for idle words
of the leaving of *parricides* behind and no other monument
as if there needed to be another as if any other monument were needed
this is the father's world it won't die father's voice won't
don't want to don't want to and have to have to talk about father
Marvin was shot twice by his father on April 1, 1984 in Los Angeles
Marvin was shot twice by his father in his father's house
yes if you linger and tarry you will be sheltered in his house
in his house are many mansions in his house there are many parties.

# 6

Shared term between last song and this song the term is mercy
when you call on him for mercy father he'll be merciful my friend
Marvin knows when you call on him he'll be merciful
when you call there's response it's that old call and response
call and response of the father's voice sound of the father's voice
"sound unites groups of living beings as nothing else does"
united gathered by the sound of the father's voice through Marvin
groups parties of those gathered brought together for the lay
house full of people from which no one as of yet has gone out
people in the house of the father's voice father's voice won't die
where did all the blue skies go is a question they can answer
went into the house the blue skies went into the father's house
the blue skies went into the father's house mercy mercy me the ecology
people call for mercy and there's the sound of the father's voice
blue skies call and there's the smooth and zealous sound
call and response of the father's voice sound of the father's voice
sound unites groups of those who were living as nothing else
ah things are what they used to be ah what they used to and ever will be
same as they ever were give Mr. Byrne some credit same as they were
there has got to be a way Mr. Byrne's burning down the house
Pointer Sisters are burning they're burning doing the neutron dance
the house won't burn the father's house won't burn down to the ground
Marvin's in the house Marvin knows when you call on him for mercy
call and response of the father's voice sound of the father's voice.

# 7

Oh feel it feel it oh everybody feel it Marvin knows that's alright
he knows that's alright people oh when we're loved by the father
the father knows that's alright Marvin knows that's alright
everybody feel it at the love party of those gathered brought together
those gathered by the voice through Marvin's voice to be laid
sound of Marvin's voice good to party fun to party with you baby
sound of Marvin's voice the thrill is real and it's oh so good baby
Marvin pronounces "thrill" so that it rhymes with "real"
Marvin was thrilled and fascinated with the idea of tarrying
over and over thank you Jesus until you feel your face being eaten away
feel it feel it everybody the thrill is real and it's oh so good baby
Marvin feels there's only time for praying and for a love party
to pray is to stop asking is to be silent to remain silent
Marvin sings the lord's prayer on his "Dream of a Lifetime" album
the singer has been hooked so very smooth that he hardly feels it
those gathered feel the thrill of the father's tongue against their teeth
if you let him Marvin will take you to live where love is king
Marvin will take you where love is king the king and his secret life
love four times in a row love four times so smooth and so zealous
listening to Marvin I want to cry it makes me want to cry
like Edgar crying through his babble song *I smell the blood*
isn't this ironic you probably can't help but feel superior
there has got to be a way and there is no way out of the house
I'm a witness wandering not praying wandering in the house of the voice.

Holy to be wholly holy is to be wholly the excrement of the voice
the excrement the stinking fruit the stinking darkness in the low cars
to be wholly holy is to be in the low cars in the train of the voice
come together people got to get together to be wholly holy
you've got to believe whatever lingers and tarries is sheltered
there can be a train in the house there can be many trains in the house
you can pull the train at the love party of those gathered together
those gathered by the voice through Marvin's voice to be laid
sound of Marvin's voice good to party fun to party with you baby
you can pull the love train baby right on honey right on
you can pull the love train baby and you can repeat thank you Jesus
one reason Marvin loved his father was he offered him Jesus
Jesus left a long time ago said he would return kingdom to come
he left us a book to believe in we've got an awful lot to learn
Marvin says we'd better believe it Marvin says we got a lot to learn
we've got to learn he is returned kingdom to come is kingdom come
this is the father's world this world won't die father's voice won't
we've got to learn it's too late to play dead in the low cars
Aretha sings "Wholly Holy" on her "Amazing Grace" album
Aretha makes up new words to go with Marvin's song as she goes along
moving and grooving with love doing and fooling with love
Southern California Community Choir behind her it's not doo it's who
it's not who it's *oooooo-ooo-ooo-oooooo* so smooth and so zealous
if it could only be that night silent night across the nation.

# 9

Heartbeat rhythm of the bass heartbeat rhythm across this land
Marvin said if we stop if we listen to the rhythm of our heartbeat
Marvin said we'll hear the rhythm of the father's voice
the sound there before Motown sound of the voice before the bass
if we stop long enough we'll be gathered brought together by the voice
if we stop long enough we'll be laid by the voice that lays
da-*duh* da-*duh* da-*duh* da-*duh* da-*duh* da-*duh* da-*duh* da-*duh* da-*duh*
that the heart would be torn out da-*duh* da-*duh* da-*duh*
heartbeat rhythm Marvin said his church lived within his own heart
would be torn out da-*duh* da-*duh* da-*duh* da-*duh* da-*duh* da-*duh* da-*duh*
the way they did his life it makes him want to holler
Marvin thought they were the lawyers the lawyers from the government
Marvin thought cocaine was the boy who made slaves out of men
it's the word and child who fixed Marvin's mouth it's the father
it's the father who fixed Marvin's mouth his father in his heart
in the Chicago Museum of Science and Industry there's a model heart
model heart to walk in children held by their parents
what the children hear is da-*duh* da-*duh* da-*duh* da-*duh* da-*duh*
listening to Marvin what I hear is da-*duh* da-*duh* da-*duh* da-*duh* da-*duh*
listening to Marvin I want to cry it makes me want to cry
listening to Marvin I want to holler and throw up both my hands
like Edgar under the weight of this sad time this same sad time
I'm a witness I'm wandering not praying in the house of the voice
I'm wandering not grooving wandering moving on the wrong beat.

# Spencer Selby

## Summit Pass

Memories of the arduous ascent
resist the higher sphere or order
intended to destroy an outgrowth
which our famous negative left behind.

It is not an accident
that an offering of freedom
is based upon a universal principle
that counts as fantasy just below.

I was outraged when you threw my letter
out the back and said I'd better get lost
to words you only signify
when you're in a generous mood.

Dark night forgets the payoff
that we lock behind a useful door,
structured always by authority
in the background of an obvious belief.

More's the better if I say so,
if I stop prophetic privilege with a word
no longer endowed with market value,
the meaning of a festival,

the first hour of real recovery
in a conversation that I'm happy to restore.
One gets the feeling of being very close,
smashed right up against a challenge

I must build and never qualify,
as if my heart alone could rescue outer forces
from their game. God made knots
that circulate this battle for all to see.

A sound gets more deceptive by the minute—
a weakness from your childhood prayer
wherein enemies discern its disappointment
quite enough to judge your skill.

Nervous pulse-like character
meets an object of ordinary sense experience
swayed by opinion not yet received
in a majesty of popular form.

Trouble puts the guilty hand on hold
with knots that bind disparate averages together.
My repertoire bespeaks disaster oozing appetites
twice as thick and half as strong.

I stand in harmony seen from a mountain-top
that's expended before my conquest
declares its sign. Memories say I cheated
in the passage where I'm most myself.

They ask me to withdraw
and just as quickly I refuse their claim.
I wait all day upon a deep conviction
understood always beyond the ridge.

My patience will exterminate every answer
which my burden can devise.
Within the darkness and the light
the steps I take discover what I have done.

## Battle of the Covered Sea

Shadows sometimes die hard.
The so-called projective tests
of personality make use of pictures
which stimulate a subject trapped
beneath the frozen idiom of night.

You walk there where there
is no choice left to resolve.
All modern illustrious candor
structures opinion somehow outgrown
to bring down the status left vacant
by ancient countries that your
thinking hardly ever represents.

Destructive rage thou speakest
lives in the prison-house of logic
you must answer through a
strange allegiance or an
instrumental project held fast
beneath the truth you relegate
to some ruined semblance
of what couldn't happen again.

If limit prescribed a broken rule
then you would be its analogue,
so sculptured to appearance
that the pencil lines it leaves
to block your path shall fare
no better when distracted
from their current job.

Time's loss is an easy thing
to think until actually stated
in a clear-cut encounter
with the evidence above.
A paradoxical word is linked
to nothing quite as lively
as illusion would have you desire.

Say who's hanging around that corner
or you'll have to make the climb
seem hopeless for the rest of the day.
Never enough hands to free
attention and behold directly
what you seek to designate
by works unseen till backed
by specialists many years later,
times hard and times you don't recall
moving in the same direction
just to approximate something more.

Which doesn't mean what it should,
I'm afraid. Not as long as you're
pushing this struggle between two
questions that have one answer
in the middle of your darkest eye.
The music of discovery has brought
you here, but that's not enough.
Starlight pulls at the rope,
shoots another bullet shaped by
memory to examine what it killed.

Both sides open then they close.
It couldn't happen but it did.
Illumination built a fleet
of warships in the desert
that's surrounded by all you see.

The orders are going out:
take no prisoners show no mercy
leave no signs unaltered in the spirit
of their instrumental way.

Like always only more
form figures where you live,
eliminates regalia while it's waiting
for the changes that survive.

# Tractor Feed

On the page I've written
how much demanding fortune
always fails to include.

I see a language
which stares down the borders
that build up opinions made over

thru man's propitiated resolve.
The difference I remember
is striking some new obstacle

for the purpose of exploring
blankets spread across the future
colloquial slang or use.

A living aspect must be qualified
by no other reason ground down
upon a context so concrete.

Chance encounters look the wrong way
at my livelihood of work and play
made timely as a subject

in its present alternative role.
Continuity of prejudice
requires antagonism toward my effort

to understand what is happening
with a short-term hammer
that is pounding below my reach.

I say whatever exists is a place
encouraged by words to bring
the end of a quieter day's response.

All knowledge under my discussion
excretes an atmosphere of hunger
in which sober talk is impossible.

I turn my back on various names
that splash their tools and methods
across the endless country

where I teach myself to live.
Construction of my value
shapes a challenge by the minute

that arouses sufficient material
to fill a very large house.
By the time the house is finished

every inch of visible wood
might be commensurate
with one unfamiliar experience.

Each room is quickly surrounded
by the map I've drawn
to give its premise an active design.

Light bulbs in every direction
appreciate twice the usual
pressure applied against my argument.

Black clouds gather in the evening sky.
Bodies fall silent in their foundation.
Experts stop what they are doing

long enough to open both eyes
on the function of a ceiling
now excluded from my system for good.

## Last Name

Could there arise other insidious whispers
of timing accepted as proof felt or seen,
mystified at having enforced a real surrender
on the many hard fought battles you must
worship from afar?

Ask no farther and laugh at what you see:
memory's tenderness has evoked a spirit too
quick to harden and too slow to accept defeat.
One more day rules the moment like a flickering
light whose sole treasure works itself back
to a point where love first crashed upon the
spoken shore.

On that spot in buried truth two dark and
frightened eyes begin their period of long
imprisonment. A rare fate remains hidden
among those bodies filled with promise when
your sentence is denied.

Up close and personal brings disorder to your
lips with more accomplishment than you might
imagine would encourage or protect the existence
of a motive that only pretends to consider such
an unthinkable need.

Timeless secrets sit in judgment just the same;
the clearest take they have on the subject
favors destruction of the utmost gravity
summoned to a point of warlike walls that
stand hard and firm for many years and then
suddenly collapse upon the stairway of your
newest dream.

One black flower blooms in moonlight shining
quietly for a purpose which begins in flames
and ends with a flash of scrupulous despair.
A most ancient solitude straddles the limit
drawn on by a meaning that seeks to escape
certain cold lips pressed against the other
side of the mirror.

Modern methods of speech activity come to
a stop. Two very different negative moments
reach the middle of your heart. A shadow
above suspicion states the terms of your
surrender which you try to put in context
once again.

# Platform

It would be better if I could remember
the difficult challenge stuck in a time
recounted beyond all relevant delay.

Likelihood and defiance
shining outward across the blackness
which no reason ever illustrates.

False start forced to remain silent
while your fingers excite sensory motions,
pull back lines of the second window's

desire to win paradise from unjust effort
you remember in coincidence replayed now
as if its warmth emanates from other

voices lighting up the unprotected grave.
And can't that mean I love you
as a world I can melt away as costly

indulgence of all sides added together
at the very moment stepping outside
history bangs and hammers on your head.

Don't you drive that message thru a limit
groping for unnumbered centuries,
beloved of itself in classic metaphor,

told with a truth not saved anywhere,
pushed aside by language
which no narrative shall ever forgive.

Another version of the same story
would leave your answer baffled
by being thrown into a glare of light

stuck between a line and a point
indifferent to its rescue
and certified destructive either way.

This logic so pleased your forecast
that now all memory must dote on pleasure
turned visibly to sickness at the end.

Admission by whom all other thoughts
are mingled with their host, danger
from where each circle gets its blood,

stop thy judgment with the deepest powers
you can muster, make the dead from
living passage struggle to withdraw.

Walk right out over and above
a platform which you never believe
should stand on the evidence alone.

# Martine Bellen

## Poupée

"in the morning there is meaning in the evening there is feeling"

Asleep with her head in her arms a small room without corners. It's to make sure things don't get confused.; She wakes every morning happy, come noon she feels lesser and by night fall One arm is different, length, different color...

Who is it that has us formulate the questions presupposing an answer somewhere to be found? The sphinx who riddles thought into words or the polluter who holds up the mirror to everyone's nudity, searching for scars, breaks on the skin, slight reddening from rubbing?

opponents of ocular evidence believe in the soul or bethink before

in the morning there is meaning

in a dusty antique shop there are piles

---

They disappeared her
Some restaurants may not be entered

Inside not even empty, he thought, not even existing to be empty, why didn't I see this before, he thought, some restaurants may not be entered, some have been built to pass but never enter, he thought, that's how some things are

---

what does it mean to be breath-less? to re-member? Some words may not be entered, imply innocence until closely examined, apply innocence gently—did she or didn't she have breath when breathless? and was she attached or detached when remembered?

---

First there was meaning, a chaos or meaning, and then feeling a chaos of feeling and then neither meaning nor feeling could be differentiated.

He asked her what she meant, but she said she was feeling too much, too many feelings to know what she was meaning.

———

flight of steps or doves

———

his crotch remembers hers

he calls her fish because by looking at her and feeling her you can tell where she came from and where she is going; this clarity of her nature is most frightening

he calls her and she answers

he calls she picks up

to come must be regarded as an explanation

the flight of steps flies from her like doves she can be gigantic, born before gods and gossips, where truth learned to be withheld, held within, shrunken head, more valued than illusion, more veined

they disappeared her but I remember her breathless

———

cognition is not knowing about things

———

In the morning she decides to give her bottle away, the act of passing through one stage and seeing what she was before and saying I no longer look the same, feel the same, want the same

awakening to say, I no longer need the same things

the illusion is less valuable

she drinks from a bottle and wears diapers. Men no longer want to enter but fly from her or revere her, pass around her watery door

———

she woke out of her dream where one night a man she met briefly was touching her inside and the next night she was pregnant

one wakes up with meaning, sleeps on feeling, wakes with mucho meanings, sleeps on feathers, doves as stairs fly from under her arches as she climbs, feels their petals on her soles, doesn't understand, can't stand on them, then falls against meaning/feeling/meaning

we really ought to free ourselves from the misleading influence of words.

# Absolutely

How far have you gone this evening or passed between remembrance other? The vacillation is ours, pure, not land outside the sin fenced in.

What makes it space, a trace-wound wound around hide so far back that she carries her body through it with the notion there is always something behind: A memory, a confused constellation, a white substance of which the heart cannot take the purity and cannot be conceived out of this world where her deepest errors steep suspended on gossip and even if she stays awake, shift in placement occurs when air's gone astray or the spirit's sent off without flesh; for there is nothing so fearsome as no image and no thing to recognize we near.

In weather she is timid since last light finds a way down to set free from above and turns away tidings. Always an absolute span as it curls out of her, withdraws, while snow accumulates, must mist over a moment of loss that is an image, not meaning, and deflection of passion is depicted by drowned river or heaving sea. If she were a bridge drawn between two spans of spirit she'd be walked over.

Field of identity sustained, still part of the entire surface, a kind of thought that walks through her into a snowy field; she is all but a ghost, and he can talk freely about matters outside her. The more she fades into the woods the sharper her outline and dimmer her concupiscent flesh. The words spoken about home automatically enclose in the roof or framed by windows while she is climbing a tree and can only be sought on branches pointing to what isn't known. Into the recess she freezes needles, needs breath no longer and footfalls of small animals replace her but she accepts this as the part of nature she'll never be a part of. Acts can be played in absence and the world is that much changed.

When done in a glow there might be an estuary that lay ahead.

Safe inside magma, the blind daughter and her brother with translucent skin feel no whether or which, just wet light lost to the clouds. With a telescope she brings it into sight of escape and who the devil also compels, pointing to the line from his heart and his private parts in the brain where we buried him so he could begin in a lone direction, already canonized for admitting the most souls, flesh-shed and supine. Each one masked so she could recognize them in herselves—their motion and sensation of sound in encamped concentration.

You try to remember where you came from but with each step there is less trace to your past.

After he steps on her wrist, disturbing her intravascular volume, ocean closes up, though he can't cry in her high concentration of salt and peace. Anywhere is the same and motion the distance between everywhere he is not. Nor does the distinction between earthly and celestial bodies become obsolete with the acceptance of flight and the possibility that what he sees or where he is could be other; the alteration of something into else makes self-evident identity is not a relationship between objects. She could not be seen before he saw her, though nothing allows us to conclude he sees by eye.

, and how this body relates to where it is or the bodies around it.

She is the wall of water from where she sees. Before her—a window with solunar ice, behind her is devotion. Before her are bare trees, behind her the world starts from what she imagines. She's not sure they are eyes though wishes he were present to know the snow casting shadow melts into crests.

Her land has this sin in it but not that one though the sky overarches and turns it around as she holds herself out into morning and names its possibility toward back thinking where she exists already as a stranger lurking to loom wonder in suspense.

When sketching, she takes the pose of her studies to understand their feats, falls to her knees to feel the flame around him, and in charcoal, draws the ashes to her fingers, scarred as she unlearns years. It is already simpler. She can turn all situations into pictures on paper and question the possibility with the irruption of speech. If she conceives a body as its movement then something else exists that depends on her life and greater, more complex bodies in mission. She can't think of his name without changing shape. There is much outside the facts that concentrate into questions through three incarnations and many miles of motion. Across the way a friend is wiping with a photo of Ceausescu's blood.

She can answer to where spirits and ideas have an absolute exterior existence, where space with trimmings out of reach absolve her, but even if what she sees is not correct there is sense in that we always conceive another who is greater yet never satisfied.

If you turn to follow your markings the tread has all but been erased,

After falling out of the forest he forgets all secrets, forfeits cards and earnings. He has memories of feelings but one cannot hand over a promise of the sun and its arrival with mauve strokes, the color of liver without delineation and the inside of her. An amassing of images, of magic, passes away and right or wrong fade from a bruise. One need only proximate experience; death flounders around skeletons, is attracted to light like the buzzing. When the dutch door opens you'll be able to answer most questions.

before you a trace of what night might come to

Without warning her home became dangerous, tears from other parts of the train she traveled through and observation intersected into infinity with written women; it is the nature of scattered memory; it is the privilege of reentering renaissance and finding herself in his pockets of flesh; it is important to analyze how this particular feeling is composed and then dissociate all persons and things so it is only her own. The spectacle is doubly visible if her footprints are carried away and pulled into her pieces as she bursts from east to west. The gaze disappears and they diminish.

and is trampled upon by an imprint that was once yours.

Looking through a window one thing is sought and another seen, so what she sees when she looks at him has two heads, little to do with looking at the window and this she is aware of but it's right before her on the other side. And she knows part of it is a secret and can't even be saved, and she has to be, and she is in him breaking laughter with the danger of mixing aspects from a real realm with what exists in the other, so that some characteristics seem so plausible she passes over them while some bring her straight back into parts of herself that couldn't be recognized around the eyes nor does it affect the body, but only the feelings made possible by the knowledge of things invisible. Movement influences passion and property too so the snow falling everywhere makes him an ocean away though why the eyes bulge in space where there is little nothing to see has not been explicated, yet she believes that it has to do with the theory she could ride light to his face and know him by reflection only. The soul has to be made desirable

it was once yours.

# Eric Wirth

## There's a Limit 1

Tar supper
white-line TV
asphalt sleep
rules hair-perceive
by half-light
to the extent that such
comparisons (or contrasts)
gall in stages

It's OK for your
thoughts to be private
taper to hibernation
between me and that
which is redundant in
conjunction with prearrangement
we leaned a mannequin
against the coroner's door

May all be well
I almost taste
no call to treat
drowner chocolatier
as shoveling out
glad to
brighten hope
cellorphaned . . . cyanotic

Flowing under heat
cutting path to rind
removal planet speaks
through authors it wants off
   Though not an author
I'm one of the few authors
that can pronounce *auteur*
what follows lying down

The regular
husk that running
naked mole rats
break in on in blind staggers
a beauty needs no apology
if washed in courage
those already here
those who will never come

I paramecium
you living fossil
said and done
only may I first
know your sayonara?
anyway pampered
aye lid up and
livid in higgledy

Of saline kissing
you can become
a votary
in shiest raw
propelled witless
before the assessor
when you're full
flavors mix

Settling the mulish or
selecting a digging stick
with startled movements
and misbuttoned shirt
you'd serve as angels' food
ack—the distortion of
personal fouls, which
day glow is

Prettifiers vaunted you
per capita with both
appetites dressing the ulcer
may I relegate
vulsant apostates in every
sense of the word
end points of a wieldy
confidence interval

You love to concentrate
sow too heavy to turn
point-by-point mating
of circumlocution onto
human adoration
and duration
now that we are here
can a beauty be critical

# There's a Limit 6

Pretense onus clocked
in one direction
overshot my wad
my interest wears
a crappie's face fed up
with all the acts
requiring jokes
no longer will laze

Influent diagnoser
and nurser
have to stick around
due to my investments
and those of my pet
salt buddy
with caudal stump
and vestigial pelvic fin

A slob mistakes—
now my hands smell—
his breathing for cadence
per therapist
I'm prevaricative
I think she said
if there are other choices
and there are

Nothing clear in mind
teacher or lasting
in its passion
when you put
it that way
   Generically a biter
I was cut uppity
a gastronome a belmar

Churlyard
though linking barracuda
face to satin skin
licenseholder
will renew
those who look
on at selvage vesicle
who prime mate

Haul off having it
both ways backed up
with the premise of egress
fallen from the idol dodge mold
as you run to tics
   After curse
you drove opener up
the envelope's spine

Novelettish to the
last imagination
of my kind—nodworthy—
hot horse
sensical, headling—
not on parole
I got "jake leg"
tauten leash

Totality does force
quality of size
of reputation in
sucklebed I like
steady, deposits
we are forged,
formed, to commit
then to forgo

Pileup of good sentiments
we're lawyers
in the book
bellicosity
ensures stimulus
of boiling point
incendiary likeness
intoned before dormancy

Overmedicalized
even the damned
visit a scientist
in ghoulishness
though the shock parade's
concealing nothing
defines the medium:
you had no right

# Because I Promised 6

He say he want to lock you, loving a heel
so the uglier one spits with envy,
and my advice, since you ask, courts order:
stop cutting silver from the spoon.
That is, I'm told, soon you get
a scale about what'll mold or muck
your world—having jollied what dabs
swan stencil I can tell fake fits.
"How many, please?" How many times I've stared
across that legend, a synapse away from
coregulation, a grit under lip line.
We, can, collaborate, my feelings hurt.
The on-on lesson for artists
who thank first can be likened to
a torrent I was wondering you
can explain?, cabal to pollute a find.


Along the same lines, today's typographers
have shot sick spunk in the letterforms,
their treacly grins recall flan
running on fleabag walls or bring to mind
beasts on mothers. Don't get me
started on parade. So this to swim
every cut burning a 99—have to draw a picture?
As I do. Dazing I always getaway liked
us, spiders speak of their webs. I returned to
stringing concertina wire with the initiates.
"Finance company"—yeh. Swathe yourself
oversold overchampioned, say your
weight, mockery accretes a personality,
that of typography, in which you
speak whenever you want as if waking
before dawn on deadline day.

## Because I Promised 7

The kind of thud that can backhand the
most-personal-fluid distemper—
rancor, an ambrosia—doesn't get me wrong,
and, humans, what else remains is easily
answered. "Am I sick to yearn to
laugh at medical protocol of tranquillity?"
You may care, but you don't say you care.
Higher taxes. Increase the taxes. New
taxes. Will live out my century but
won't cling beyond all usefulness. We are fire
victims, and more philately it was worth it
to flame like a portent for once.
Erotic fog burning off by noon succeeded
nightlong lizard airglow in regimen
of resins; showers are free. Do married people
kiss? Thank you for not saying the obvious.


One day I sat downso long, bathroom lock
in. Sometimes you know that your ideas tow
the song of an eel hurled down the alley
of glory. Tomorrow—for sure. I live
in a home and can't conceive components
having past and future in unguarded hour;
just know laws. Who here controls what goes
in me? Pouting into a periscope revives
learning in its hives. Sweet, I coughed
from rule and could begin to register
your curiosity pin. Keeping weasels
from pants and detonating standing syrups
go hand in hand, link surprise
sweats to manure dust. It's noble not to
bad-mouth—gist of hell. Won't you resus-
citate my love . . . however, I shun pity?

# Todd Baron
selections from *E Y E*

## prelude

denying love's consumption, come to the gate that feeds him
the watery touch . it is not echo's shadow or the ending of
beautiful words at one with the beautiful picture, but image
denies him the ease of his mother's eyes, reflection not shadow
rejoiced in his grief   knowing the other's false nature
wanted nothing but self nothing but countenance
a circle of white petals' effigy serves him confusion
& mourning lacks trust . there is no modern fable
now that belief will have spirits away . the same dangers exist
as repentance is briefly a dream, likeness is merely depiction
as such is a soul who asks who is watching & written & whom
disdained in a hoped for virtue, false & true
becoming external, who are not imitation's eyes
are imitation's eyes

## untitled 1.

moving these scarlet letters untitled
permanent sway it is him not her
as though meaning were loss but pure color
astringent ploy delicate mouth
you've done nothing but recover removal
past being full & counted recounted (like) glass
comprised of nothing   trial malignant order
air enmeshed with movement   nothing grows
in a sequence of doubt I see
the film that sees me   the mark that consumes
signs like a ghost signs like a ghost
offspring shoots forth past my wanting him
eliminate each rock that shoots forth
origin sequence outward unbound

## untitled. 2

like parallel dream the eye plunders to get up
that lasts not out of self but stays the same
same calm rigid head the sky of my shell of sky
"clot of anger,"   my life isn't it
a verbal ebb   the last shingle like perception's dream
the divine path foreclosing sound
here and there a chair for hedonist open
lying to myself what may be delivery
too soon then waking up a field like yours for want of
nothing less   less time devoted days nearer sound
then saying I'm too soon fixed as
lies   lives   no sooner than

## untitled. 3

towards the light   the always repeated light
airy delicate facile origin or absolute whole
a language bought in facsimile permission authority
experienced in want reproduced by need that
something said   I'd have anything but this
vacant invalid champion this waking up to morning
as any sight or single entity entropy artifact
dim tethering can't even open the book for indecision of
images even the undemanding breech having been left lone
& unfrequented need it speaks itself
my sight my mingling voice complete

## untitled. 4

anonymous impoverished under thread
aannulled as if I hadn't happened
surrender past sleep the pale gallery knowledge
that nothing is perceived assured the eyes the head
the mouth ears again eyes drowned in comprehension
comes an inlet a loop as lips sealed
are sealed in prescience   crest appears first sub-
rosa or human subordinate (to) (a) mortal world
opens and shuts my door adrift on need
past tense went out went out into the garden
to watch myself exist

## untitled. 5

behold transparent house how like a fixture forgotten
unseen for the likes of what & where
alike a greater fee for living estranged
in certain dissolute light entitled not to see
impressions withheld yet not in mimicry
that made a section of you end
awaken I address all this time taken
under not as tender   know the opposite confused
bright transient pearl dripping as a captive drips
the core of substance assemblage semblance of

## untitled. 6

come to bed like a grove of stems from the bottom
& go out   go out arriving
interim of break at the crutch of life
that's given work from a table of crockery
moments of calm gravity not weight or austerity
but the face that rides the byway the blossom
& crooked bloom aggrieves the wandering pass
as psalms assemble over inebriant song
cultivate fodder farther father customs all ways
a path of stalks stuck in the rain
embrace solitude not hate the self nor end
not even age he could not serve   receding haze
rushing to the pool began these letters

## **untitled. 7**

I can't escape the mouth I'm in
Between the seer & the deep blue sea
The mirror'd road
Opening route the muted tone so clear it's
Overheard as hearing
Bone white teeth   bone 'neath skin
For feeling hurt enumeration
Waking from a book   the book
& kin would hurt myself
"the world I'm in" holder holder home
A good thirst or a bad one, equilibrium
Not grace, what takes so long
Stretch of Song

## untitled. 8

you gave a lonely song   paradox / contradiction
the border-song octave sestet negligible to some
by far beside a wall not rimed foreseeable future fable
a crystal replacement point by far
more temperate timed exposure
never probed your dulled monotony find me
find me strong if I would walk to this door now
would open with a concrete god impending waste
the horn of scarcity released the wind
the wind developed brevity . oasis mocking air
primary strain set clean & dark & black
reducible chant once that words devoted
dye of hand fixed motion parts across the page

# Jena Osman

## Venice

traces in the ivory lead him out. he is the last part of a trail which you have followed. his path is due to the whims of your conception, a ribbon on a pole. with years, the gradients are tested, the steps that happen on the shifting plates—such movement only told, never felt—easily replicated by a diagram or gesture of a flattened hand. every inch of his manner indicates a stumbling transition; a desire for simpler planes.

having met you, his face appears more doll-like. is it the wind continually howling or your growing need to lie down flat in your own preoccupations? the sun itself refuses to reflect the everyday. instead, small steps click through the metropolis. this place, an oven to your foreignness, breeds a certain formality, he is swathed in those robes. he seems thinner, his expression changing according to the light.

why follow any further? you know everything he will tell you. certainty of his disappearance is what keeps you grilled to the activity. day in and out. the box had a special significance, but what it was is mostly lost. to hold an object representative of a regal idea. now the memory is lit by a small bulb in a much larger room.

the pole fits down his back and leads to a balance. he spins the perfect plate at the end of a stick. you notice, as he boards, that the legs have been incorrectly carved while the water vessel hides its purpose and he digs the ditch further. you feel if you encountered him in daily life you'd be quite sure of the next steps within the box. are the physical things in place? have they been marked by the eye and left there to sit? you wonder if his breath had been diabase (a city), would his disappearance be less clear.

## over-painting

oarlocks of the parrot
within finger bract selene

she contains the fossil horse
the opening of a human history

her palatal blade
her own red tail

epaulette tree, chaste tree

parrot turns a cheap-jack peddlar
she an axis in the axel of the flowering glume

tembrel umbel


surface:
ORNAMENT FRINGE SHOULDER
MILITARILY BLIND

her body in red winded over
persist blaze up to the hat

yet stay there

the crawling losses up against the pane
tatterdemalions extend towards doors

regalia beach and bracelet inflammation

her wings prismatic but singular
catastrophe of open light

the red cast of her back
denying all subject


surface:
FACES CUTTING ALL AXES
DISPARATE SENSE OF FUTURE

do not pressure the hands
the shard-licks of flickering

a shoulder lost to its shadow visual
almanac of presences

grasses, sedges, spikelets
not here

to meet the carving to meet variety garnet
to meet the gateway anything short-lived

alteration of quartz
her gaze stressed phonetic


surface:
POMEGRANATE
HELLISH GARRISON HOUSE

shadow plates out in front of her
dissolution curve of her bent back

also in remains

she the blue trillium
belonging to a discarded system

baritone this sallow this vacant study fossil

she alters the facet of her arm
indication of zephyrean stress

she a deep variety within the pokeweed
irregular polestar


surface:
A FILLET-CROSS BETWEEN THE FLUTES
BORDER WAR

deny exposure
this dress not a dress

equatorial of her white side
singing chatoyant

lying on the jackstraw of the blue bed
lining the canal of the spinal cord

she bootlegs the clear astronomy

uninformed birch
no household

arranged by wind free of branches


surface:
VICTORY
PALIMPSEST

# Jerry Estrin
from *Rome, A Mobile Home*

## Counter Song

Damaged Frames (holes in the museum roof), the
 whispering
of the background whoosh.
A performance, the fortress of the person on stage.

There is science fiction.
There is an outlawed transmission.
Our bodies outwallop any transmission.

There is movement on Tuesday, budget codes and
 responsibility
of your thighs, unprincipled, uncompleted surplus, the
sources our principles are our red revenue sources,
 accumulating.

Laws are feigned, oedipal.
Each law of contempt implies its opposite, nightingale.
I can lie in your sense or between your teeth.

The idea nature is transformed.
There is foliage and the wind and fucking, shades
landlords, charity

concerns us.
This is in real time, and no long range.
There is Tuesday, budget codes and responsibility.

Incongruent crisis management—
A system of blues lies under you.
Arrangements of contractual gestures.

The park is uninhabitable.
The soul is unfathomable, a deep peach
of dream speech ensnares depth.

Each curling flower is between spaces.
Amphetamine has smoked marijuana.

Flares are the early Renaissance, the eye.
Bush Street is near Montgomery Street Chinatown.
The junta is in Chile.
People have often said the city when they meant
    capitalism.

Consider the park as an order of language, a green.
Israel knows what God is from what He is doing in
    history.
A man is dancing to static or he is being shot.

Our static is rich
a point of view
Your point of view doesn't belong to you.

Humans are traitors to their species.
Random violets in the park.
Park a premeditated park.

\*

One makes a portrait, perhaps empty, of fated being, in resistance to a crushing symbolic order. Writing takes its primary measure of this constricted, if artifacted space and time. A phantom order empowers its own existence. It is a hope, or a false utopia, a neutral territory, a blank milieu.

\*

There are a hundred sonic booms in the valley a day,
    the people.
They are camping on bombing ranges, the people.
The land is legal because it is contaminated.

You find yourself in a position of power.
You can think, the land is regal.
You are participating in reality.

They have prejudices against artists.
Seeds of scurvy-grass growing in waterpots.
Their rooms are filled to excess with art objects.

The book the just language
of the park, one more metaphor or another,
spills

reverses its horizon into me.
Cite the way why
argue it, those wise don't

inflict your living this place
simple, quite, kind.
There is no neutral landscape.

These facts have to do with the truth.
Do you believe in the truth.
We admire the brilliance of the least fact that happens.

Believe in the porosity of the existing situation.
The light is incessant, the eternal
spring enamels everything.

A park comes into view only for you.
We have worries.
We have the same reasons we had in 1929

to flee from reality.
Visualize the poem's door.
In which sun are you asleep.

We are fascinated by an absence of totality.
If anguish is embedded in the territory.
If there is no Palestinian territory.

There is fate.
We will be acting out your comments.
That which never has preexisted.

The snares are relentless among the worldly.
If the air in the city has preexisted this city.
If the park is an ongoing effigy

Our words are not autonomous.
I speak
like all your friends

or any of your friends talk.
Talk.
Talk makes me feel first class.

Thanks Merrill Lynch and Co.
I know this ironic time
and that this line

is leering at us.
Us fears are their features our
futures have become mutants

because all future representations are futile.
Save the box and the memo preserving it.
Preserve what has prolonged you.

I should be your comments
to transmute an education.
We should fuck and fuck

because we will all be literal when we fuck.
Fantasy is clipped from living material.
Responsibility is unjustifiable.

The verdant fountain of the Tuileries.
In the park the fountain.
There are obstacles and malevolences

which are contradictions.
There is the board of trustees.
Bequests of land round the capitol.

If there are enough caricatures
There will be an equivalence
of distortion.

Listen on Friday we will get metaphysical.
We will send the document to planned parenthood.
Wilderness in the notes.

The Capitol is alive, harmony
keeps acquiring our targets The park
Responsibility is unjustifiable.

Separations are our responsibility.
My airfare I'll be sending you.
Keep silence. Silence cannot be kept.

Check.
Their documents are secret.
All documents are secret.

Who is organizing this surrealist show?
Our parallels are secret.
Fall into the person you are

an endless suffusion, profusion.
In the mountains drive fast,
True intelligence would be to flood

an enemy with true intelligence.
Torture his linear consistency.
At the border visit the rides

like Walter Benjamin
with frictional curiosity
one can cancel

an interval in Mecca
caress injuries
teach

each creature to be a monument
calling through time.
In the park a stone fountain

weeping out our years.
Our union exists
amid permanent damage to the replica.

# Johanna Drucker

## Deterring Discourse

### Mutant Politics

Newspeak language drops the ballast of reference. The politics of communication loses its credit rating. The realm of representation threatens an invasion in the name of humanitarian aid. A controlled discourse grabs onto the edge of critique, holding the peephole shut against the light.

The virtual stalks its prey, arriving on the beaches with the scene already set. The refusal to speak the obvious maintains the taboo against knowledge. Our information has become a nation underfoot with a brightly lit sky above, blushed with the warmth of familiar surveillance. Hard wired into fact the casual services of bodily functions refute the claim to individual personality promoted on the screen. The legislative body, nothing like the outmoded physique, took leave of its senses without regret. Our protoplasmic meanderings were thrown to the small feeders, who overheated in the economics of waste. Consumption passed us through the social and out into the ecosphere as gas. This was still a dark continent, coming up on the edge of the millennial horizon.

### Genetic Knowledge

The unsaid, the uninvited, and the incorrect: all cast out of the social network. The forms of transgression are permitted to make their own fashion statement. Time after time they date each other, closing in. The tightening circle of dead silence paralyzes the facts. Her dreams are scattered before they are spent. The bank account of rugged individualism had closed. The fertile waters of revenge rose to stamp the woman's face in the shape of a grin. The program had been aborted, but not its effects. The epistemological formulae threw the happy days of ancient childhood up to mock her. The open marketplace for the exchange of sentences was shut in her face.

In the closet, a soul— accoutrement to another outmoded ritual. The cost of resistance had been lowered, in fact, as the price of complicity rose. The need for recognition short circuited all attempts at revolution. Change had become an earnest longing, a transformative effect, charged with nostalgia. A world which could have been was measured out in intervals no mathematics had the heart to reference.

## Conditional Present

The fabric of our lives unravels, our eyes not yet accustomed to the improved light of a new dawn. Handwritten lines, produced with shaking limbs, crabbed the small letters into bad attitudes which they would have kept to themselves under the influence of another administration. In the cherished climate promoting perfection surface values were continually under inspection. Cash was put down, but there were many more days to spend than could be accommodated under the old account. Time had become fluid, disorganized, reconstituted according to the dictates of opportunity. Total permission could only be granted by fate: in that respect the children were still cloned in adherence to an abstract equality, quickly modified by the absence of low-cost narratives.

The light had been filtered to remove the bigger particles and fell unevenly on the inner landscape. The freeway strip continued to spew forth ugly looking platitudes, here projected on a big screen. The uninhabitable had been reconditioned to become the unimaginable.

## Cybertrash

Mars transit, waving in the breeze of fragile hopes, had been struck once again from the short list of high priorities. The old frontiers foreclosed on the new ones. Territory simply would have to be invented instead of gained. Two small figures in silhouette repeated the motifs of the proto-romantic landscape. This in itself was insignificant, though tacked to the wall of the lab they become the leit-motif of a new era of experimentation. The brave new system left dark shadows on the air as a kind of test trace, toxins expelled into the organic tissue of an erstwhile cultural imagination. All along the decaying hillside of history a traffic in ruins reinforced the absence of traversable roads. In the old world marsh weeds tangled in the blades of a motor made ineffectual by discrete phrasing. The exhaust billowed out into the halls and threatened the collective equilibrium, but no dream had been printed out. An older factory, grim remnant of the pact between family fortune and unmentionable labor practices was pressed into the service of romantic monuments to civilization and its outmoded discontents.

## Millennial Rushes

All fears are real, crashing through the ceiling in the order given to the machine made parts which inevitably pass for citizens in the new community. Memory swims out to meet the familiar figures of an outworn administration. Building technology had been improved, nearly swallowing our old hesitations by the tail. Crying out again and again for dignity the populace, such as it was, was shepherded into one office after another while the streets outside were wiped clean of their glands and infections. Labels attached to their undergarments almost voluntarily were sewn back again and again into the pages of diaries left without keys. Locks were opened electronically just for the sake of generating a public debate about the very nature of desire. This was not an alternative move to satisfy the whim of hard fact.

The clouds hovered on the horizon, boiling in their stew. Down below the waters raged incontinent, slapping the sides of armored vessels tight in their barnacled berths. Machinery kept its look, if not its function, in the new regimen of style.

## Total Invasion

Agency was an issue which became a tiresome repetition in the arena of new positions. Motives were taken down from their hangars and put on again to bodies which did not care to compensate for the strange discrepancy between fit and form. Fading evidence destroyed itself under the pain of investigation. The nation state had ceased to function as a kind protectorate to small investment and struck its teeth deep into the chord of resentment. The old policies dominoed into one contingency after another, while the world waited for the right moment to exhibit outrage as a form of mild politesse. This was not a question of conscience, but of strength, final and physical, resisting the disciplinary regime of love or the compensatory hand of regular aesthetics. Blood was tracked across every threshold in the client state, leaving its mark on the sunburnt faces of imported goods and staining the skin of the household gods. There was blatant hostility towards the power of sentiment. The path to glory paved its own way with intentions forged in the heart of the new machine.

## New Weather

A lazy unknown river meets her at her door. Her heart is broken from lack of action and skips a stone across the receptive surface of that silk face of water, rippling its reflective muscle against the mirror of a used-up sky. The dreams which come home to roost in the asperity of a cutback atmosphere make their bid for a solitudinous wash of experience. It won't happen there, not that night, on the porch, as the sun goes down across the bodies of the birds. But it may happen in the morning, with the arrival of the news, breaking on the shore in an unquiet rhythm. No one speaks headlines in the clutch of a conversation unless they seem to be certain that an outcome is assured. A handsome one.

The new air reminded us all of Spring, try as we did to put our energies into maintaining a semblance of reference to the old order. We were hoping for rain, all through the short morning of construction noise, but there were only dry heaves and the yearning sky, struggling to compensate for earlier misdemeanors.

## Perfect Language

Their minds bent to accommodate the unrecognizable specimens leaning to the left and right of their appointed places in the categories of all named things. This was not a question of commerce.

Harsh words fell with the impact of young lumber and shattered her mind's delirium. Picking up the pieces later she was obliged to mimic the mode of good action though her implanted instincts all bid high on a move to the contrary. Nothing in the dossier had prepared them for such intensity of experience, peeling layer after rapid layer of hieroglyphic skin stripped off the hot atmosphere which tautened over an opening too small for air. Whose message was this, breaking into their night time travels with revolting violence. The long chain of their command swelled back to the point of entry and no one knew better where to look in the oceans of privacy for cracks in the veneer than these unmotivated vermin. The generation which had spawned to life with so much optimism now recoiled under the inertia of false promises, monolithic misunderstanding.

## Artificial Nation

We went below the decks. Our humanity ached in its chains, pulling forth the creaking sigh of wood bent back against itself. Harsh reality knocked repeatedly at a door shut tight against understanding. Refuse nostalgia.

Memory asks no forgiveness for its borrowed time. Even this morning the dutiful rhythms of a hydraulic pump made their marital statements in the mixed company of much traffic. Melancholy was ordered into submission by the heartfelt exchange of programming advice. Motives were no longer useful, having been replaced by circuits. The old historical project creaks and groans, lurching on the road to a paradise designed by young conservatives. They scurried off into a violent sunset, reporting their movements on an indifferent scanner. The audience for that kind of thing could no longer be repressed into vital statistics and given away in the supermarket as a promotional misunderstanding. The flag went down on an imaginary angle between the line of sight and the sharp edge of the lost horizon.

### Cosmetic Communication

Organizing tendencies mutilate fresh air while history reasserts its video potential as violence in the home. A gentle atmosphere of celebration stalks the proletariat identity. In daily life the parades have turned the limited political universe back into itself, displaying the profound poverty of the spectacle. No one goes into the streets, which are damaged by the winds of order and the ugly handling of significant threats. On their tongues the taste of treatments came with the rain and water which had lain long in open beds beneath a post-industrial sky. All the richness of the environmental agenda attacked them at their brief game of golf while the tragic medicine was peddled to the strong corners of the weak earth. This was also a time of mourning, and deep wounds refuse the suffocating balm of sentiment which even dulled cannot manufacture a knife's edge of pain from the lived space of the real. Time becomes substance by the absence of access, emotional reference closed in, on itself, the unspent portion yet to be invented in a form which could be readily consumed.

### Proverbial Difference

Elections were falsified according to the perceived nature of events, that was logical as reportage fell short of its charity goal. Dull days and violent exercises bespeak a military mode, entering the field to break open the fragile pores of carefully husbanded deposits. Out on the field they lined up the smallest among the children, who were also among the brightest in a constellation of celebrities whose artifice had long ago expired. Impersonating the past they were sometimes reinvented with the vague intention of violating copyrights and sometimes merely for the indulgence of necrophilic flights of fantasy. On an actual roadbed the formerly utilitarian image of the innocent landscape fell apart, disturbing the archaeological silt of a once familiar form. A backyard stash of ritual heads, result of a statutory decapitation offered great possibilities for restoration. These are physical facts. Excavation into the flesh would provide no such rewards and no opportunity for reconciliation. The residue of politics scums the blades of a fan installed to break our concentration into an oily sweat.

## Hypergraphy

Nothing was forgotten in the steel-trap memo of unspoken codes. The fiction of the unrecorded voices was excluded from the archive. The image on the wall could speak, it turned out, and not just about family secrets, but in a manner so baroque the laughing stock of history was the butt of all its monologues. The curtain fell on the spent display and the residual silence asserted itself in news taking flight as the final broadcast. She let fall the pencil of nature on a receptive surface which inscribed the particulars of historiographic moments in terms of a filament theory of progress. The gasping air valve of a broken machine speaks in tongues and challenges the right to due process in the metaphysic of appeals. No one left alone with this equipment knows anything about what to believe. The new menace of speaking arrests development just at the limits of regular programming so that nothing, really, can happen to keep the nighttime terror from returning as the heartfelt communique of efficient aggression. Oh, the exhilaration of the life we could have lived had history been willing to fulfill its mission and just repeat itself obligingly.

## Virtual Referent

Festivals held in the name of sovereign principles went unheralded by their real motives and flaunted their unspent legacy with gratuitous flamboyance. Looking away her eye caught on a telegraph line and went modern, breaking visual syntax into hard-edged fragments as she struggled to enumerate the very laundry list of passions on which the people's authority had been established. The race was not against time, breaking the frame and loping into view on the screen of a ruined amphitheater whose claim to space went right back to a religious era. The need for public visibility motivated everything and worked as the generational motor for illusory, fantasmatic and hallucinatory productivity. Knives to the heart, a twist to the ending, hostilities cease and then the problem is to live with the militant hypocrisy of peace. The tanks blow up along the road, blocking the sight of the sublime, a careful strategy to mark the backs of our hands with remembrance in the name of the old habits of tattoo. The final judgment day arrived without the attribute of keen salvation.

# Beverly Dahlen
from *A Reading*

to amend is to make up the difference
an uncountable noun
good advice but not several furnitures
filled the space along the west wall
a nightmare like a fiction
not a real dream
pursued along gothic lines stone stairs
the weight of a soul in the balance

cross that out counting
and not counting
the bone china to mother
the gift of retribution

what would make it up
though I have not charity
I'd be as tinkling brass or
field lilies
who are the poor *in spirit*
who walk around with the kingdom of heaven
in their heads

who'd be there counting out *peoples*
*kindred* in the roofs of their mouths
here is the church
and here is the steeple
mimicking past lives
the ghost of a chance
the productions of time congealing
the trees swaying in the wind
as they do in silent films
at 16 frames per second

over and over a tardy light
resurgent insufferable
*until a way was found to repair the shield*
our poor spare orbit
among the splayed 'aggregate of
gas, dust, and stars' quoting from
existence the movie
the celestial omnibus parked in the alley
the old conductor an allegory in a child's garden
of verses




the basis of a grave philosophy
whatever we think to think
the 'ghost of a chance' an unearned
speculation
the moratorium on interest
bearing steadily to the north




meanwhile the trees
their mechanical boxes grayed out
the stump of a tooth incised on the tongue
where *poco a poco*
we are returned to the void
piece by piece released to decay
on the verge resisting
the panic urge to *noli-me-tangere*
the blue-eyed doctor bearing down
calm abstracted
rifling the wound

laying up treasures on earth where moth and rust do corrupt
she switched into her substantial marble dress and golden
teeth and earrings                       whatever next
in this progress towards *everything*      unfitted
the veiled allusions wafting in the nooks of the afternoon
whilst one was accorded a private tour of the food
stretched out across the room          forgive us
our debts that stringy chorus of unseen voices
wrangling in the open courtyard        'the celebrated
pleasures of the mouth'               *trust*
must be another indulgence of those privileged to wait
in cushioned rooms but the poor believe nothing but pain


and what *to entice* o 'temptation' he laughs
leaning to the left a known word
the lisping Spanish proved out he leaves
for home ahead of time                  *Alejandro*
my
no relation                               father and citizen
                                           escapee
as indeed who is not
a replacement

in your old age surrounded by grandchildren bearing arms
for los Estados Unidos                the desiring machine

on account of the bad blood between us
I'd furnish your ears with English
an agent of the state
this is the language God speaks
naturally

no known tongue can capture the necessary lesson
this pit of excavation we call our history
the temptation to *everything* dragging forward
the tortured arguments                the final cause

there at the beginning the blank page the *tabu*
*la raza* chalked on a board in the kitchen
the interdiction of the north
wind as if the belly of darkness turned
over cows hides fur leaves
their undersides            an edged light
the sounding city a nest of serpents

the logic
of the prohibition of one a detour
where nothing
intervenes absolutely
the end of it
a run of time




fortunes flower
abruptly



not so much the
                                       signification
        that would
what's                               matter drifting un


              such that we are at least




crowds probably, more than enough
crowds, probably more than enough

the next thing you know


all the trappings of winter set out on the hillsides new grass
a charitable heart                    unabated an old welling
towards the spectacular              a festival of light
how ever the dark resists it we come indoors to the fallen
logs in the fire      the diminished voices




here let the record show
a figure built as it proceeds
a pattern long on justification
short as the days shorten
willy nilly to think of Stein
at the head of the column
weekday service here to stay
wandering among the hyacinths


labyrinths shall we not?
*detailing* the cuts
to disappear
may in Spanish also be a transitive verb
as 'they disappeared my son'




the interrogative meets a fuzzy blank a settled indifference
a soft defense the unlikeliest events as you'd say the only
creatures in their masks backgrounded all making shine of it
the moon a pillar the children with their mythical names
in the underground the faces of the blind gods stare out

across the tracks the train arrives in a storm of wind
rustling our books and papers together adjusting the headset
wandering *with all the biblical antecedents of that choice.*
thus I use you.
the exact price the bird of prey gnawing at the vitals
the renunciation of pleasure on the way to grasping it
the perception of hands in the creation of categories
bestowing on things their *-hood*edness
as a quality or manner such as velvethood or cuphood
so I came into wordhood at an early age sitting right here
don't you suppose we can speak of such nervous organizations?
and now a second cure appears and flows in the path of least
resistance that rebel and thief Prometheus emulated far and wide
a little learning is a dangerous thing who would renounce that
power once procured?




awake at dawn underscore that balmy and listless a sinister image.
a tropical storm standing in the way weather permitting.     walk
out gathering execration review the setup one last time nipping
into winter's weakness. nothing follows.


*Even if we ignore its merits as a work of literature,*
*the book seems destined to create controversy.*


no error. she was sitting above the shelf someone said what nice
perfume but she wasn't wearing any a wholly resistible object.
downpurse relevant wind a stone in the head on which to strike
the rhythm. a world demystified and made over a new theory of
ghosts. beam me up.


of the parts rational of the whole mad my voice bouncing off the
moon. just here she said you go into hyperspace.

renegade information gatherers select a code. recombinant DNA
working close to the bone reset the eye. hand to mouth re-
suscitation standard English in disarray.


orange flower water the soup's in us. the captured stick thrown
over the edge of the cliff numbers of ghosts multiply. the space
in the train taken up with drumming. against the background of
industrial waste the nostalgia for the tribal




burning up the distance
listening in to Santa Fe
you could be anywhere south north


can we speak of the local a day in anybody's time zone nights
tipping toward the solstice hemispheres of execution remote
events written in the fossil record written in the stars
remote execution of events speechless for the luxury of life
on one continent.




for the luxury of life on one continent
Africa *thrawn*
Asia *thrawn*
the mythical Americas on the verge
a storm of penitence arises
giving the devil his due

tall in the saddle Armageddon's cowboy
rides out the night
workers of the world unite

*

September 29-December 9, 1984

# Susan Gevirtz
from *Anaxsa Fragment: Coming to new land*

**The Lands**
> *arrive on foreign*
>   *shores*
> *return with momento*
> *to the land of our own language*
>
> *of the matter*
> *for thinking*
>
> *they persist in coming—wait,*
> *forever wills*
> *to go forward*

the fragment or remnant
photo momento
or raiment

> Always raked dirt courtyard of wave
> lines settle in shade as thin curtains blow
> out over cool tile floor. Scratchy sketch of seagreen
> and seaweed brown walls. Wake to face of hands memorizing
> a torso the way fingers on a tumbler learn ice.
> Fluorescent lens of sand mirror
> underfoot. Fall in. Fall to

He must have spoken. Whether he actually mentioned is an
open question – where

**Landlock**
I now realize the abundant and majestic love my family has for
me. My Father said, "You must dress for the occasion." I have
finally discovered who I am. I am their son. I live diligently for
those to come.

> *This is the account,* Anaxsa, here
>   it is
> *Now it still ripples* warm, *now* it
>   *still murmurs, ripples it still sighs,*

*still hums and it is empty under*
your *sky*

*just let it be found*
            behind the shade pulled
            on noon sunlight

Then comes the borrowing, the counting of days,
the hand is moved over
    the boiling of water Anasxa
    even that a different matter

## Landsend

On two legs in herds travel. Carrying translations in bulky valises. Raising the spout high above the cup when pouring. We learn that height alters taste.

I call you across for clarification and adrenalin. Did one actually speak? Anaxsa—put on your headphones. Lend me the danger lodged   in your appliances.          Still warm, it hums
under your empty sky account       ripples it still sighs

## Landfall

Time draws near. Notified in semaphore. The access approach, beware of too much. Backdoor ajar. By what authority does the sky address us thus? What shape in this slot on a form for writing what? A portrait of waiting back to back. The unproven conjecture of airports as doorways, regarding herding capacity and habits. Table manners.

Let down, let down the sky like mosquito netting

Under her dress is something
that matches the hotel decor
Mexican bordello style
its red
*gathers and secures*
*all disclosure*

It is red dictation
hand over mouth
the fullest speech blinded

speech   broad hand covers eyes
*Sacrifice yet again, even do it to yourselves*

**Land Of Conceal**
immigrant translators, conductors   all pass in

*proximity of something unsaid.* Roll over. Come here.
Attentively tie knots of limbs. Instructions our overseer. Talk
fastens deliverance falls from ripped seams.

*The arrival and departure of whatever has arrived.*
*They experience approach and withdrawal as the basic trait*
*of advent.*

Is this the threading of tender command through the eye of the
seamstress? Give me your body parts all out of order.

**Land Of Evening: Above Ground Episodes**
*Into what language is the land of evening translated?*
Purwokerto, Central Java: Two fishermen went missing
five others were injured when their boats broke up and sank
after being hit by wave in Nusakambangan waters Cilicap
yesterday Suddenly big waves hit our boats

>   live off the fat at a price
>   under quilt of tropical night
>   cavernous restaurants, strings of bulbs,
>   grilled fish eye
>   plate white
>   vault of sky

*our relation to the advent of destiny is gathered in this*
*departure*

>   brief reprieve
>   wave noose or bonnetted
>   rescued from their original plan
>   whose parameters
>
>   like a marriage
>   continued to occur
>   to them

*Is there any rescue? Rescue comes when and only when danger is*

Its saying    Its announcement    An instrument
A place called ibal    a book

    go missing
    spar under and relent
    airless avoidance
    at node of turbulent
    behind swift below
    disbelief test in
    contraction
    void mouth
    in which names are deposited
    to be eaten later

*This is the nuance*
be warned

*The first two figures seated there are manikins, put there as a joke.*

    something said
    has gone amiss
    like fruit cracked open
    on lips of fever
    no swallowing gets
    sweetness to
    leave

Depart    Sunar 18    Sander 20

The seaward
Anaxsa the landward
woven bamboo
the word or word
miniature floating raft
takes the taken
to be counted

# Mei-Mei Berssenbrugge

## Fog
(written to accompany a dance)

1

Hundreds of millions of years ago, days were many
hours shorter.

All things, sounds, stories and beings were related, and this
complexity was obvious. It was not simplified by ideas of
relationship in one person's mind.

Paths of energy were forced to stay in the present moment by
being free of references, making it impossible to focus on two
things at once, and showing by its quietness that energy of
attention is as much a source of value and of turbulence as
energy of emotion.

As lava burst from the ground to cover the planet, it also freed
water, which escaped as massive, billowing fog, a contradicting
ambition of consciousness to acquire impressions and retain
strong feelings.

Fog is a kind of grounded cloud composed like any cloud of tiny
drops of water or of ice particles, forming an ice fog.

Since water is 800 times denser than air, investigators were
long puzzled as to why fogs did not quickly disappear through
fall-out of water particles to the ground.

It turns out that the drops do fall, but in fog creating conditions,
they are buoyed up by rising currents or they are continually
replaced by new drops condensing from water vapor in the air.

Their realism is enhanced by smoothing away, or ignoring
discontinuities in the fog, for images of what we really see when
we travel. Beautiful, unrepeatable, fleeting impressions can be
framed only within the contradicting ambition of her

consciousness to acquire impressions and to retain her feeling, a way of repeating a dream.

Large areas of the sky change from totally transparent to nearly opaque within a few minutes, although throughout a lifetime, the night sky appears remarkably constant.

Showing what they are without revealing what they are, paths of energy are transformed at the moment before their dissemination into an empty field, like dew you see on a spider web when the sun hits it, after there were spiders.

2

There is a great wall in the fog and rain.

There are some mountains in the mist.

There is the line of a wall in the mist. I go in and out of the fog on the rim trail, and the mountains rise in fog among yellow leaves.

There is a veil of fog between her and a sunlit flank of yellow leaves.

Slow whirling galaxies allow stars and gas to fall into hot disks of matter, orbiting around massive holes at the centers of the galaxies, allowing a branch to spring up at the moment when the snow melts from it.
Your concentration is interrupted by a shadow on the periphery of your memory of her.

Your concentration is a large array, where debris in the mind appears as an intense shower of heat radiation, like a cluster of instincts to the body.

3

As far as the transparency or relative compression of her boundaries is concerned, and your backward focus to it:

A white glass of water is hard to conceive of, because we cannot depict how the same thing would be white and clear, and how this would look. She doesn't know what description these words demand of her, since she is alone.

She can sometimes see the events of a story as if they lay behind a screen, and it were transparent, rather like a sheet of glass, since human beings can be reflected on a smooth white surface in such a way that their reflections seem to lie behind the surface, and in a certain sense are seen through it.

4

She can describe for you the phenomenon of feeling her way through the fog. For whom does she describe this?

What ignorance can her description eliminate?

Which person is supposed to understand her description, people who have been lost in fog before, or people who have lived on the desert and never seen what she would describe?

You can be trying to connect the experience of being lost with something external or physical, but we are really connecting what is experienced with what is experienced.

So, when she tries to talk about the appearance of the people's feelings around her, she wants to connect how it appears to her with what is solid around her, but

she can connect appearance with appearance, how people *seem* to feel, and their communicating with each other within this appearance, from one person to another.

Is it possible for four different people in this way to have four different spatial concepts within the crowd? Somewhat different ones? Different with respect to one or another feature or heat inside a building, such as armspan or eye contact, and that could impair their mutual understanding to a greater or lesser degree? But often hardly at all, like ice broken up on the sea.

From above, I can't tell what distance away it is.

## 5

It has no shape or color that is stable, as if I had fallen asleep and a long bridge appeared, where my relatives are like companions crossing a bridge.

Her friends and family are like people you meet at the marketplace.

When you look at your husband, you think of a floating flag of the roof.

Even though he is your husband, he is not stable. Anyone believes what anyone says about you.

This is a realm or field in which other people exist in subtler forms than the body in daylight. A part of the person can become visible at a time, or parts of the people, and other parts rest in folds of the fog, as if they were muffled sounds.

It would be hard for you to believe that anything within the cloud exists.

His body, which you do not see exists, having dissolved its cells into a body of a cloud, which shifts in and out of focus.

It would not decay.

The body is the space of the point of a moment in your seeing him or hearing him.

You can calm yourself by moving toward one of these points, the way you move along your own breath.

## 6

You could try to make some fog into a piece of white cloth. This is impossible. Though it is visible, it is not a concrete substance. She tried to make a delicate cloud into a cloth. She could not, so that is why he is staying here.

Or, she could try alternating dissolving in the light with dissolving in the dark, for speed.

At night, she could see as if the country were illuminated, as if it were day. She could see each person's face clearly, and she could remember if she had ever known this person before.

Dreams cannot disturb the fog or you, because your environment has no territory. There is no territory in a fog environment.

7

Lack of clarity within your environment is tormenting. It is felt as shameful. We feel we do not know how to even out a place for ourselves, where we should know our way about. But we get along very well inside buildings, without these distinctions, and without knowing our way about the decrepit structures.

In any serious interaction between them, not knowing your way about extends to the essence of what is between them. What can appear emotional is caused by the emission of energy out of her body, which you feel, but there is also such a thing as "feeling something as luminous,"

thinking of him as the color of polished silver or nickel, or a scratch in these metals.

8

This fog in space and light and dark is analogous to the solid ice of a very pure environment, and how it cracks and gets water, from one stage to another.

Its area of wide space varies in lightness from place to place, but does it look foggy to her in the darker places? The shadow that a cloud casts is in part darker. She sees the parts of the space that are farther away from the light as darker, but still white, even though she would have to add black to depict it.

Looking around in her room or any wide space in the evening, she can hardly distinguish among the people around her, and now becomes physically frightened of them.

And now, illuminate the space and describe each one you saw in the mist.

There are pictures of dreams in rooms in semi-darkness, but how can she compare the people in these pictures to those she saw in semi-darkness?

9

The bright light slows the senses. A picture of the space in bright light, as if etched by a laser, can slow your sense.

When we see or experience something with the senses and the senses get slowed, we can stop at this object, for example, a person who is beautiful.

As soon as we see this person, perception is blocked by the desire to go towards the person, with the misunderstanding of fog as thought, that just runs on and on. Her awareness is completely lost in distracting clearings of space.

10

The sky, which illuminates everything we see, can be gray. This can be true of someone around you in your family. How can she tell merely by its or his appearance that gray isn't itself luminous?

Thinking of him as the color of polished silver or other metal.

The fog of the way we feel our way into this focus, seeking by feeling, lies in the indefiniteness of the concept of continuing focus, or distance and closeness, that is, of our methods of comparing densities between human beings.

Is foggy that which conceals forms? And does fogginess conceal forms because it obliterates light and shadow, the way light obliterates or shadow obliterates, also?

Black does, but fog doesn't necessarily take away the luminosity of a color.

Darkness is not called a color.

11

The first solution that occurs to us for the problem of the appearance of another person is that ideas of actual feeling, instead of the appearance of feeling refer to points of tiny intervals or patches in the other person.

How are we to compare the feelings between two such intervals, simply by letting one's memory move from one to the other? If you do this to me, if you remember me, how do we know this feeling has not changed in the process? If you do remember correctly, how can we compare the feeling without being influenced by what has happened since?

The way we call a complex of intervals with which you depict the family member, his emotion with respect to you. As if the person were a piece of rose-colored glass.

Would he have the same emotion in a crowd as a piece of rose-colored paper?

A storyline develops based on your moving from one breath to another, and you start to want to continue it, like a span of good health or exceptional beauty. You want to continue it forever, and your memory gets involved, in how you perceive the space around you and the human beings or descendants in the space.

You will eventually feel so empty inside, among your family and in your memory of your family, that even while you continue breathing, your breath will not bring volume or space into your lungs.

12

They counted her more accurate and more inaccurate memories as black and white stones.

The more accurate memories turned out to be white on the outside, but they were unconditioned by the desire to form story out of her memory, continuing story, the way we wish this space and light to continue.

Therefore, we appreciate the fog, as the power to make the space continue beyond the single perception, into raw material or youth of the body, like a body of light.

It dissolves now at the top of her head, now five lights into her heart. Now, it dissolves into her body. Her friends dissolve into light. They dissolve into her family, which seems to dissolve into clouds that were already full of light.

It is not so much the quality or brightness of light, or her understanding of this light, as the number of times she dissolves. The faster she can dissolve into the space, the better.

It is almost as if the complete dark would be ideal.

# Hank Lazer

## H's JOURNAL
## III
June 22, 1990 - June 30, 1990

81-Though I hate equally the notions of intuition, inspiration, and imagination, know each to be fraudulent ad copy for self-aggrandizement, I myself work intensely (and best) by principles only partially known, at work by a method at once constructed and resistant to formulation.

82-"Far behind me they rest without bursting."

83-The movement of the text from the one written at home to that complicated social and financial negotiation which may result in a published product is often a deliberately neglected setting and season, attention being directed to a more pleasing vista at hand.

84-, "What's the matter?"

85-These longish sentences display a tropism of sorts, a turning toward (and into) summer's long days of extended light and heat.

86-"It got up alarmed and trotted about on its long large legs, and even nibbled a little grass, and behaved altogether as if it had been an inhabitant of this planet for some years at least."

87-As I do theoretically (which is inseparable from breathing), I study the roots of St. Augustine to determine whether it is a fungus or cinch bugs responsible for the brown patches.

88-"America's best writers have offered one another the shock of recognition but not the faith of friendship, not daily belief."

89-The azaleas long done; still a few hydrangeas; plenty of day lilies—mainly orange or yellow—and this day, against an unusual (for here this time of year) blue sky: blasts of crepe myrtle's fuchsia blossoms.

90-"They get three cents apiece for them, not boiled."

91-The mayor of Tuscaloosa stands by his proclamation that city workers may not microwave popcorn in the Municipal Government Building: the seat of power shall not be made to smell like a movie theater.

92-"I feel that I am there only by sufferance; but I love to go by the villages by my own road, seeing them from one side, as I do theoretically."

93-Adam (or is it atom?), I name the plants and animals, I name all manner of things; but the names overlap, and some sound the same & give way to puns and play, and anyway I love nicknames, and to change names (as time passing yields other perspectives); so what is it that I am mapping?

94-"Where I turned up to go to Scusset village I saw some handsome patches of *Hudsonia tomentosa* (not yet had seen the *ericoides*), its fine bright-yellow flowers open chiefly about the edges of the hemispherical mounds."

95-When what is being described does not yet have being, then the language of description becomes another thing.

96-"The piping plover, as it runs half invisible on the sand before you, utters a shrill peep on an elevated key (different birds on different keys), as if to indicate its locality from time to time to its kind, or it utters a succession of short notes as it flies low over the sand or water."

97-There is a different sheen to sticky leaves of a pecan tree or shiny awkwardly large magnolia leaves when viewed in an era of stockpiled nuclear weaponry.

98-"Anyone who can speak can say the words, 'Thus saith the Lord,' as God is always finding out."

99-The sureness of the sentence, even as it confesses doubts, lies.

100-"In a genuine Cape Cod road you see simple dents in the sand, but cannot tell by what kind of foot they were made, the sand is so light and flowing."

101-To travel or to voyage, a journey, as a means of settling oneself; to theorize, as a going away and a returning to, but changed; such are the allegations, though the same might be claimed for staying put.

102-"War is like art because it must deal with calibrated space and the conflicts of partisans."

103-At some point the morning yields to the afternoon, and the writing of such sentences—until late in the evening—becomes impossible.

104-"Everything he can list he is putting in his book; it is a record of losses."

105-As if the regard, literally the attention, of one for another made the former feel substantial, important, worthy; so, nearly two-year-old Alan says, "I *told* you."

106-Once we abandon the notion that we must make the reader say "wow" or "awww," then we have, in spite of the loaded words, entered into—well, precisely through and in those words—a mature relationship, one of more sustained attention, in advent of the freight of such particular words, an adventure we may now embark upon.

107-"See apparently a young bobolink fluttering over the meadow."

108-The flickering of moth or junebug at the lefthand edge of my field of vision, sensation not unlike what I anticipate as a return of attention to this sentence a few years later—dim recognition of my participation in it, a vaguely familiar somewhat off-rhymed inhabitation of it—awash in a broadening and oddly comforting forgetfulness (which sometimes we are foolish enough to call progress or development).

109-Is it system per se, and its visibility ahead of time, that converts idle and attentive activity into work; and is the mystification of not-knowing anything other than the guarantee of an invisible harness?

110-RETURN UNBOUND JOURNALS HERE

111-To read in many (          ) at once.

112-It is difficult to remember when a dream, an ideal, a way of living presented itself as purely inviting (and I, or something that goes by such a name, assented to this one).

113-"In his youth his temperament was fiery and so to correct this he adopted measures."

114-He sits, comforted to think nothing needs doing right now.

115-Next door in curlers seventy-five year old Maree totters about and inspects where city workers removed underbrush from the far end of her yard, tells me she feels sicker than ever and in an hour or so she's to throw a party for a friend's eighty-fifth birthday, says she just prays to the good lord that she doesn't fall out; soon, the street fills with large white parked cars.

116-Time cannot be thought but can be thought about, or thought in, while thinking gives some compass to it, and even a particular pace and spin.

117-I am writing a journal; surely it could be verse.

118-Sings Alan after supper: "row row row your goat     gently down the street     merrily merrily merrily merrily     life is but a dream."

119-"What happens instead is that men mythologize their forces, as they always have, project them onto demigods, and then serve projections."

120-I write with no anxious grasping after: sooner or later, what I am doing will come to me.

## PLACEMENTS 4

unbidden yet is   and so and so   a dab of black
it was never easy
               · dangling angels
                              flow to the brain
that eerie temple


.


seizure or singer   silence and whiteness   demand (is) an audience
it was never easy
               inventing steps
                           apply a compress
warm across the forehead


.


the shocket blessed   and cut it   unplug is from the socket
it was never easy
               white walls and
                           fresh registrations
cascading fuchsia bougainvillaea

# Elaine Equi

## Brand X

I know you think
this is about sex
but that's only because
it's really about advertising.

Someone talking
in an office.
Someone comparing two things.

I make decisions
or my body
makes them for me
and certain nights
everything is perfect.

Wedges of light flap
slow as Indian summer.
A red receding.

There is real violence
but it's an after-dinner violence
mellow in the air
as sex is a kind of violence

like anything
that pulls us toward it
even though we're unable
to ask for it by name.

## Before and After Speech

Troll-like
...in tufts

something other
than silence
surrounds my words.

To follow
unwillingly

with belly
and lip
thrust out,

to follow
the unwilling

thru the silence
of the room

and the silence
of the page

(mere conventions)

as if language existed
"a dis-figured voice"
outside the body

to be poured
from one container
into another

—the illusion of it!

# Destinations

### 1.

A hand
leafs through
autumn

with a logic
that shines
like oxblood.

Every morning
I don't hear it

the absence
behind the bird.

Nudging the frame.
Singing its head off.

### 2.

Your letter
is full of energy

as though you were
inside a color
a whole flock of them

but I slept
on the day
I was born

and see sleep
as others see the world.

A lamp filled with
the oil of dreams

hisses, stone chatter.

3.

In brine daylight
thought becomes brimmed.
Fraught with sudden
steeped in listening.

The jars
around which presence
gathers its virtues.

To inhabit my walk
(though a pleasure)
and all that that conveys

(limitations, frames)

This romance
of going from city to city
with a lamp.

## Reading Akhmatova

Sick and reading Akhmatova.
All afternoon
cups of tea

then into the larger teacup
of a hot tub.

Half of me
feels ethereal
while the other half wonders

was it really possible
she spent that much time
falling in and out of love?

Somehow the aftertaste
of her words
makes me think
it was more a career choice

and that the bitter
medicine of her poems
is directed
not toward the lover
but rather the reader

who forces her to reenact
the same scene
saying over and over

"you are the one"
"you are the one"
"you are the one"

with only the
slightest variations.

# Craig Watson
from *Reason*

watch out
though couldn't be a darker daylight
seeping in shivers, thickly
its tasteless fluid cupped too long in the mouth
across black field, icy film
and crusts of shadow drape
on mouths of objects
even crow won't land, won't speak
will break and fall
so can't get beyond a certain point
while drifting up through saturate sleep
toward the surface of seamless glass and silvery static
address a continual preface to explanation
don't want to ask the old questions
must do so, over and over
until flat against wall or shadow
dropped by a deep, hardening sky
now stand close, full frontal
limbs apart, tensed for embrace
can't move from the inside
though coiled to spring up and forward
into the liquid pane

still there is
or should be
in one detail
one word
the promise of middle ground
struck still by equal opposites
in solid volumes and seamless minutes
then look at things too closely
and begin to hear a length of distance
spent speaking while spoken to
or have to ask twice to ask for
the shadow the shadow casts
because moving devotions move away
into the skins of silhouette

where you unlisten all names from things
or answer a question with a question
mouth-to-mouth until empty
and think
is every silence failure or a voice
lost in the speech of the statue
its stone wind in a glass desert
saturated
naked and opaque

alright, a word
then another
but only a gesture
to mark some sounds
that extended hiss
of a crystal dissolving in
the same syrup that formed it
lying out there in frozen graves
sliced by roots
and brought to air by stalks
in the clean space of ideas
where there's nothing to say
that doesn't take the form of a teardrop
rounded softly at one end
a bladed thorn at the other
people say they roll
but actually they launch
then pierce
or explode
on skin
followed, of course
by the same dead laugh

you create a voice because you create a mouth
but who is speaking
words simply fall out of exhaustion and go about their
    explanations
like bats flying through fire
this close to the wall, their sound comes back again
so there's a certain powerlessness
because the fulcrum is not to control
but to maintain

as if the purpose of thought
is to see that all possible lives are distilled

who can decide for this
even if the world is only a pattern
repeated in arms of suffocating thoroughness
in order to survive, to feed, to dwell
this choice, this product
this darkness, this threshold
sudden and terminal
salved by the numb
its hovering soliloquies

be careful what you say
after all, you are the one talking to you and
even certainty appears in halves and curves
maintaining a precision to this featurelessness
which forces you to think twice
to discount all destinations
to speak
from corners to islands
from ice moon to black sea
from richness to meaning
as if a nightmare were an accident
as if the body was the child of the body
as if you could actually have a body
as if it were possible not to consent to the apparent
as if it were understood
that words are spoken from
the mouth of other words
back-to-back
to-the-wall

the mistake is thinking that something is what it is
or supposed to be
hands resting behind back to make a temple of
   afterthought
as if mass stands for infinity
in a representation of tables, candles, trees, fingers
which penetrate the liquid public
where each dissection sews blade to its path

except it *is* literal
subject-matter-in-real-time
luminous, decaying
into one organizing fact over another
so that slip stream, that wake
extracts the noise
in which the familiar is the part that repossesses

in this way we say what needs to be said
even though there's no one listening
but they will nevertheless hear it exactly

perhaps speech is a kind of mathematical function
of what it's possible to say
given the givens and minus the contingencies

or a kind of clothing which variously reveals and conceals
the form of the figure
unself-correcting

Or is there a greater emptiness beyond *emptiness*
as the sky is 'full of stars'
dismembered from the shadow of sense
attempting to reason
haunted in detail by the inheritance of each act of acting
until the realization of already having become
cathedral and tomb
cold whispers
in the rust of noise

# Joan Retallack
from *ERRATA 5UITE*

vowels pristine     (of)     spoken rhythms you are sure
  of it?

perfectly     that explains why they


page 89, Julia Steele "Untitled"– last line missing:

  My parents were really royalty

read read for real if men spit (res) upon ras er- first go halfway to set in motion inset for suffixed breast motion of aberration solo eyes do not hear (her his) (his her) dislodged utensils insist on liken elbow to Old Norse *angr* grief erratic for 5th aug/dim/wheel/column/klang for kling in farbenmelodie

read need for read arising from the phenomenon of color p lies in a plane of 3 points *svdig* to *svidg* to *sdvig* having only letters and silence in this written form *ar- *or- *art (a) exist for exits [should have been noted] man[sic]kind[sic] & you shall followed by 5 blank pages (b) to be spat out later

read for for four last line misting eart aron (of) spoken rhythms untitled add a pronoun what it is/has agitated to a strange and not (for) tensor analytic reads as reads as follows crossing fōrd for Emerson glad to brink of fear ybore dislodg-èd enso semi amazia o tics of zero sum ergo blather to rush to race to wander read for for fore *tu* (large bird) errorious to be in motion *o tu cara scienzia mia musica* varied as were mixup agitatur not known the man could not swim & now apostrophe s restored to pronounce ritual formula punch in code for teeth (love 's savage splendor) read land and math for lang and myth 's urgent isosceles smile

read foretaste for phrase could not deny Struggle against Misery part of longer work (*res*) in Old Norse rushing raising casual doubt 60's postulate #5 read this is for his is read ba (bha) bay read basic works of Aristotle for sun's missing particles once chiefly fig now arch defacto lush as were

His Words in her heart rather than upon her lips (A&H) correspond to an old need so authentic modern works are criticisms of past ones (A1) beloved by the gods and as such he [sic] (A2) So much for Tragedy and Epic poetry (A2) *hominum* [sic] *dabit homini* [sic] *A te petatur, in te quaeratur, apud te pulsetur: sic, sic* (A3)

A&H-Abelard & Heloise/A1-Adorno/A2-Aristotle/ A3-Augustine

read for for read read forehead for missing biographical note for our read out read this category meant to include now cut cut error whole she Tokyo they origin for any number to become zero if you are in the right system a) or a) against or a) afraid as in a) growing not to but where in yr personal ergo she she again

read should read section 2 line 7 lake 0 in one of those on Mr 'see (Upper rt left read Mt for Mr S for 's in See professor of foods and nutrition grazing sheep on front lawn of diagram 4 at end of preposterous claim should read other or once understood he said be sure to mention I'm local *cum* for *sum* (*ma*) la la logical

read note on figs (body/rouge/mind/noire) for what reply does one make to oil dependence as music for Gesamptkunstwerk read Gesamtkunstwerk poetic verb for word this troubled devotion ewhich I had not (67-73) been singing whole moving fast almost motionless simplicity of for (seen)(faces) whose coordinates are reads as follows promised multiples whole grains green vegetables dried beans for cheese and eggs how can you buy or sell the suffixed variant sky *agher- ont line para chapter no home to go to missing up and down the ladder most harmful form to read the Chronicle regrets allreasonable dog left stranded on causal plane

should read seemed clear from the movie the sudden technicolor salute (for) (the) Chronicle regrets hiring the one who committed the error or something inadvertently left out to connect all those motionless gestures across time (failure to find defined) specific function of/or/for nature's rerun nature's unexpurgated gaze

whereby the human race [sic] seeks to recover its right over nature (B1) were possible but to learn ironically to disappear (B2) where everyone comes to witness him[sic]self really his [sic] own death in the gaze (B2) and imposes upon men [sic] a grave (B3) limitation of the causal mode of description (B4)

B1-Bacon/B2-Baudrillard/B3-Boethius/B4-Bohr

read would be too easy to suggest for emotions confused ideas imparted on this earth 's etybotanical act of love 's silence intersects intention eat/drink *eguw–* slurping suffixed lengthened form to read as follows who spits upon the ground spits upon themselves' brief solace in errata slip a wafer in their mouthes

erratums for the tummy La La Ta tin erratum neuter past errare all history lies behind before Poetique Terrible delete as/like Duchamp as Fred Astaire to read epit ess pref b iv b neut p pple sundry errats' distended verse to wander err erratic nudging **ers** root erratum rroneous erroar The World's a Book 'Tis falsly writ

er rat tic er rat tum err O Polonius this is too long an error The World's a Book 'Tis falsly read falsly printed though divinely penn'd And all th'Errata appear at th'end (1632) fo (of) aberration ers- to be a slow mo God upon His solemn Review finds not one Erratum in the Book of Nature whole as writ (look!)(1691)

read Luck read kcab upon time past Th'extravagant and erring spirit hies etc. chiefly fig now obs quasi-trans cognate object to variant res Germanic *res- Old Norse ras rushing medias race Wordswords streaming firth in fifths ers-a- to wander in causal debt errabund erroarious (produces sneezing) rerum turn to zero




errat to curiositas clubbed Medieval sin should read between one word and next the zero (led by her) I found the silent water now for le read les in holocaustes (homme-dieu) read Khmer noire in *ANGR* old as Old Norse grief and were a trouble to my dreams this earth im part (slowly through the mind) its silence




If I may quote myself: 'Art...is the work and witness...the realm of "the between"' (B1) between the various powers of man [sic] these cannot (C1) and what is human knowledge but a cortically embodied flower (C2) a soul devoted to such (C3) method which insists on exhibiting all the assumptions required (C&N)

B1-Buber/Cl-Cassirer/C2-Churchland/C3-Cicero/C&N-Cohen & Nagel

please note 24 & 26 printed upside down read dear for pear or peer reed real camino replaced with stet to let it be Molodzhi read Molodezhi O patriotic stirring verse word'swords and irony begat to bigot from *eirein* (say/ironic) agedom agedumb gnotus to ignotus nominious ig it is dominant hominy last wordword not last

read Carmen 68, line 22: pull down the (should be) pull down the house wo:m (should be) worm, the reference to color last para page meta x in error should be look back upon time past that former errata's and miscarriages of life should be henceforth suspended by the blast with what strang utterance sustained et et

for he ear hear heart earths arts knowledge read know ledge unjust defy margins true belied read should should read grue bleen phenomenon Gd/Ev (cont) (should be) (what) Prob of (should be) featureless romantic flood (should be) the point of vanishing perspective punctum a um music comes and goes without a trace

ERRATUM   p.9: truth is not nor for-not too (ergo) nor late readnot too late nor truth were not for-never past rescue inorby words'words in on ground floor Cafe EAT she by opening was rather than the end rather the or thinking of him errect ad nipoled in sweet categore of light beginning to or from what world she came

peace she read fro but for real and eleusive catagores good 'n o1' thicke for relephant classical reverence, (see Mysteries) read land o late district pull down shades 'n stirrup wordswords behind closed doors chunks o pavement disturbed ears for eyes 'n having only phrases to end each child's sentence with a pyramid

can answer the question what nature is unless he [sic] knows what history is (C1) apparent question of the relationship between fact and fiction (D1) a disseminating operation *separated* from presence (of Being) (D2) If nothing has preceded repetition (D2) we must admit that human life is very often subject to error (D3)

C1-Collingwood/D1-de Man/D2-Derrida/D3-Descartes

# Jeff Derksen

## Interface

I needlessly mapped an occasion, splitting my support, serving myself.

A north, a south pointing pronouns in pockets.

"Ordinary people were saying 'We want to be free'."

Higher Alert.

The return for refund where applicable part was never clear, but we continued, stopping at each gas station to ask.

Liberal pride harnesses a portion, and I'd prefer not to comment on my name.

"Sweet Dave" written in black felt pen on the back of his yellow rain slicker.

The fish instinctively know where the international boundaries are.

The dupe quotient seemed to apply so clearly to me that I had to leave the table.

Soviet Union 24.9%.

A pinched nerve or an upper rib took away all enjoyment of the available technology.

I was humped like a salmon.

Terminal Carpal tunnel syndrome.

"We can see a day when borders will mean nothing more than knowing where to cut your lawn."

I had been puking at the announcement but then stopped, seeing no profit in it.

Evil in a nasally way, with a hundred miles of barbed wire, but once in the workplace an agenda smoothed over the whole thing.

The structure I hate also hates me, but it makes me, and that's where the problem starts.

I peeled back the wrapping on the bag of ethnic paper clips.

The demographics preceded me.

United States    18.3%.

"Sell abroad or go under" is forced from the drop in domestic arms needs.

We sought to mollify the sulking with a buy-out plan – I could hardly hold on when it got slippery.

The black chairman of the Joint Chiefs of Staff.

A kind of horned-up atmosphere saturated the bank line-up, snaking through the blue velvet corral.

Interface of self and place passes me through a translation machine.

But when my left eye is jumping, I don't know where I'm at.

A car horn punctuates the trumpet solo.

How could I talk about a brushstroke?

Even though the ultra-sonic image of my testicle was on the split screen right in front of me, I felt detached, cube- or kiosk-like.

Through hard work and volunteer effort a pragmatics began to arise: how does it translate to I really really care about whatever.

A strike that tries to "inconvenience the public as little as possible."

The guys in the car gave a polite honk, as if embarrassed by such a coded response.

Every team has to have a grinder, I just thought it would never be me.

"Males have strange and elaborate paired crab-claw-like jointed appendages attached to the snout, which had a sexual function; the females are unencumbered."

It was a bonspiel I could hardly support, even as a decent tax-dodge.

Great Britain   17.1%.

"It's only with plain talking, and a give and take on both sides, that will ensure there are forests in the future."

The high-pitched hum started to hurt, but we decided not to say anything.

Propaganda points to propaganda within a transparent frame.

The translation process that ends with "...Harvesting the necks of the infidel aggressors."

Pure desire arrives like a train – on rails.

Seal-like, barking and clapping, tilting and rolling my head back until they agreed to take the unpaid portion off the bill.

"Urgent Fury" wasn't the movie, but the code name: Granada 1983.

It was a cynical attempt at inclusion, based almost entirely on family background – just said no to a regionalism of noses.

But once the embarrassment blew we actually talked, balking at a paradise subsidy.

Then the letter returned replied with a quirky formality, like viewing another culture from a deaf ethnographic point of view.

Something like post-colonial packaging taken personally in a resource-based economy; I look out my window and see history *versus* I look out my window and see a window.

Visually complicated, overlapping and lapsing.

Small, polished engine parts that still look usable, but which are unidentified for any function.

Bush's "approval rating" is 87%, the highest for any president since Roosevelt: February 1991.

I wanted to argue but was locked into my role of simply trying to be nice, or to conciliate an agreement, so I just tapped on the glass and walked away.

There was a picture of him "in the field," notebook in hand, handkerchief on head.

"A picnic not a potlatch."

A layered invention, looking in its own window.

That binding arbitration of lip to neck or hips to hoola hoop.

France   8.9%.

It was bad news coming even from a hundred miles away, *or* after adapting, we grew to like the rattlesnake necktie.

The percentage of blacks in the U.S. Armed Forces is higher than many other industries – this was talked about as a progressive step.

Apparently they'd been doing it like that for years.

A used car-battery sells for $1.50.

One hundred and thirty-eight pounds of joy.

It was a way of thinking about myself that took in all perspectives and appeared not to damage the environment.

Those small, see-through fish seemed a good model.

I won't say that the imperialism placated me, but that the stroking of the consumer goods really calmed me down.

And an eel-skin briefcase as a signing bonus.

"Power is frequently understood as force personified" and the pronouns disclose this.

An intensity in menus, the pivotal moment.

The U.S.S. Meyerkord docked in Vancouver before going on to the Gulf.

Oil-proof and $69.95.

I kept my head down and pedaled the machine faster, the air of sexuality getting thick.

Bright and long-lasting negative effects of Cartesian perspectivalism on viewing our own bodies from the head down.

Two elections, about a hundred days of rain and it will be spring.

It's a made position, like a pewter spoon or a leather letter opener.

The Rocket Richard riots would be an example of spontaneous agency.

"Jeanine is a living example of Noranda's attitude to employees."

China   6.3%.

This train.

The residual anger resides here (points with right hand) and accumulates here (points with left hand), I'm still looking for the spigot.

More American soldiers were killed by accidents during the buildup than by either the Iraqi army or so-called friendly fire.

Generic or genetic.

Sapped like a sap machine.

There are so many *ones* I want to be — beyond the cardboard maquette stage, more at the prototype level, the "working model" example.

A subject-in-process with a horn section.

Rent context.

By the book legally and with the compassion of the United Fruit Company.

Every device will have its homecoming.

"We may not have all the right answers, but we have the right car."

At no point in Canadian history has a federal government been so unpopular: January 1991.

Counter-top culture.

The silent trajectory of the fist gave me time to think, opened the local to a national identity with blinkers on.

Anxiety punctuated by time.

West Germany   5.4%.

"I'm a man — spell it *I apostrophe M*."

Patience dispersed through the legs lead me to "I become my job" now I'm pulling together like white blood cells.

The language of war at this juncture is an aim, a name.

If history is the memory of time what would our monument be?

The semiotics of hair show me a socially saturated sign and I engage at the primary level of meaning.

General failure of hippies.

By extension I am engaged in war, driving my car or taking one on the chin.

Non-union job structure creamed my attention span.

The U.S. Navy did phone to apologize, making me feel even more like a nation, more unlike the United Nations, but still a little sore in the jaw.

They wanted to argue generations, but the past year is all archives.

"In the Canadian Grain Elevator."

There is an incredible amount of natural beauty and we engage with it accordingly!

Step down from the cockpit and give your name, hometown, and stock response as a universal narrative.

So-called air-superiority writers.

A highly developed national sense of irony was in place by 1942: Canadian raid on Dieppe was code named Operation Jubilee.

Now I become my own lunch special.

Pin-point accuracy, with the "pin" being a building.

Italy   5.4%.

I see traces of my labour mechanically reproduced and it makes me *happy*.

A generic ethnocentrism made it "everybody's town."

The highly competitive profession of proofreading.

I took the initiative personally so sought the etymology of *basket-case*.

A life-time achievement award that doubles as an ashtray when laid flat.

I still answer the phone as if I were "employed": that reminds me that the structure you hate, hates you.

Schwarzkopf's verse, although having a clarity of tone, lacks formal innovation.

*Blowing off steam* implies a natural build up and then release rather than rage.

Like a pig through a python.

I wonder, would a matchbox hold my subjectivity?

Lieutenant-Colonel Butt phone me at work to assure me of his regrets on the "unfortunate incident" and the strictness of the naval code.

Books float.

Japan   3.5%

One abdication, two resignations, an erasing of the electoral memory and it will be spring.

I enter the artist's body of work by walking across Second and Cambie, becoming a flaneur in modernism at the shutter's click.

The body could be pure pleasure — floating in an isolation tank.

The brine shrimp of the family.

"Operation Comfort" lacks irony in it not recognizing an alternative system: comparative literature without the *comparative*.

The stacking of so-called psychological damage has me at the crossroads rather than the keyboard — manifest in tissues or fish scales laminated to a role model.

Or it's the post-colonial model that makes us humble, optimistic, plaid.

At this point, rather than tying, I'm trying to quote enjoy my life end quote whether it's eight and a half by eleven or quarter after twelve.

The bay curves past the family beach and pier, crosses the 49th Parallel, and terminates in an oil-tanker dock and naval base.

Sweden   2.5%.

Sexual activity displaces my stomach upward by an inch.

The fleshy space where the hyphen was between *work* and *place*.

Six months before a presidential election, Bush is tied with a candidate who is as yet, officially undeclared: June 1992.

*Batlics* as a dictionary entry is the victory of context over text.

I bought your book for a quarter.

My body's attached to my leg, to a genetic history, to a parallel sentence structure stretching over the horizon.

"A reader must face the fact that Canadian literature is undeniably sombre and negative, and that this to a large extent is both a reflection and a chosen definition of the national sensibility."

Cheerleading is a growth industry in the U.S.

I'm stepping aside here, just to say that if it's not my job, I'm not going to do it, and if it's not my arm I won't twist it.

A relegation of last week to a distant and unconnected past, an increase in the amount of "paid political announcements" on TV, the end of the salmon season, and it will be fall.

My world, myopia.

"*The* car is *a* extension of you."

A dread feeling, linked with time, becomes the experience of quote the quotidian end quote, so I'm a fragment reading up to see when I was whole.

A serf in his serfdom.

Operation Desert Shield, Operation Just Cause, Operation Rolling Thunder, Operation Success, Operation Martyrdom, Operation Should We Be Doing This?

Crosstown traffic is classist rather than racist.

I would like to quote jump out of my skin.

Official national animal.

"I honestly want to restore Kuwait's international borders."

The space between *dismal* and received knowledge is where "popular culture" steps in.

Post-election morning coincides with the first frost and the plants have a shocked, trampled look.

Poland   2.3%.

The one and the frenzy.

A pair of shoes on top of a rock in an empty lot where there once was a house.

I'm returning after an extensive guitar solo.

Cranes dot the skyline in a homage to the domination of *economic* over *place* – it is unbuilt business I'm talking about, the Pacific Rim lapping at my ankles.

Unemployment went up in the U.S during the war.

It's too easy to attach a possessive apostrophe to mass produced products, so I'll end here.

"Racism has no place in the battlefield."

Dominant tropes won't allow me to buy tripe.

I carry context with me and become tourism.

# Norma Cole

## Rosetta

§It was the same pattern: the shower
   of rain, appearance of ravens, description
   of the oasis

§verbs of posture, verbs of spending time

§a future expressing the will or
   intent of the subject 'I will do it'

§she said, after the war had finished

§market-minded; verbs of speaking
   making noise and arguing

§'look' for 'see'

§verbs of bringing

§following but not gone

§reported speech with
   periodic remainders

§body in glacier

§off the sea like confetti


"Blessed are the forgetful" we did
love that place. speculate. what other
work could mirrors be doing? I remind you
of our childhood together. and of
the pick-axe of examination. you don't
want that to be
stranger. tell you
the waiting

§'arrest and movement'

§there was talk of an empty city

§stuck together

§with words or sister city

§made a clear pattern of abuse

§turrets painted by squadron

§the mast's game

§ballast of gravel, sand or stone

§the stone itself, soothing

§impossibility


work done on the rock stood or fell at the
mouth then was written, *carved*

notched, grooved....

            "Broken up by rocks"
the waterfall could not measure up
                            as if they're
looking right at me.    ghost
beauty
added four parapets


*lost objects (gathering)*
*in the Empty Quarter*

*'whose work' would*         *later*
                      *throw him*
*in which that gathering*

§ear-splitting whistle
  undeciphered *but* proof
  of their presence. so he

§deciphered on the level

§*Courier de l'Egypte
le 29 fructidor, VII° année
de la République*

§the most important of
  these 'daughters of Tyre'

§way, path, groove, were those
  signs (mysterious) in their hair


...wave theory of light...the bumpy treatise...we are
...losing...linear ramblings, floors...

                                                            its calm flatness...
the broadness and shallowness...


Moving anxiety
      for the reality
moving without you. again
wrapping the proscribed
image in sheets
between
grateful reproductions

§dreaming from the

§signifying landscape X names
                    of the dead

§formed from the taking of a country

§wreckage and simple understanding

§one day 'woke up' and
  just knew how to do it

§how these things come into being
  and *that they do*


One translation says
                            Osiris says
but the other, earlier one says
                    The life of things
                    after the defeatof Typhon
                    the moisture of nature
                    through the vigilance of Anubis


The names were surrounded.

        the play of color
                cloth against the body
        against whistled monody
        recorded
        body against

They used the four-spoked wheel.

§restless

§apparently it will be
  filled with glowing
      shadowy blanks

§change going through to
  experience

§around to approx.

§'say' to 'read'


...covered...all...residues...over...a
ban on it...insoluble...surround...

> *no interest or*
>
>                       *, believed*
>
>   *it so*


posted
on the installment

    They were
pretending
reason from understanding
.   Of the necessity
of the world

§our city has done that and this

§irritation has returned

§not to speak of drawing parallels, are not always
  taking the context or implications into hand

§no        longer
  dreams  blind

§build these things and paint them

§brightly


Nothing of the past is in these...pictures
stations of the plague...


*on a silver tray you also left your card*

lazy and erased
elevated by foldings
in three

genealogy of cities, Carthage
daughter of Tyre

to place up
lacing vocabulary of action
places direction with brackish water
wind called splitter or cleaver
refusing to let the supply ship dock

§Again, I refrain from describing my delight

§faltering (they believe you when it
  suits them) where you sleep

§under the window, but what kind
  of transition occurs adjacent

§in spite of it, crowded
  matrix of those long colors

§eros well-known
  the city is in flower


## "SEE THE CITY SHINING"


*list memory*

false document.   a true
classification

and found it simple, a false
translation



*Movement is Eros, the poet said, it's*
*well known       the second dream*
*closer to our grief*

# Colleen Lookingbill

## Six Poems

### Room

She walks in walls, mirrors on every wall. Blond oak wood floor perfectly smooth, perfectly warm to the touch. Off come the shoes, socks, bare feet each toe making contact. Plaster ceiling overhead, hand swirled white rough iridescent quality. Emotional currents and just enough calm. Facing this way the door disappears, then to the side it appears again. Remember we don't want to get lost. Not this time.

It happens a need fulfilled. Hand against the glass mirror surface, Cocteau film "Orpheus", water skin feeling a change in pressure and then the other side. Three years old enough to understand privacy old enough to lose it. Now womb fills monthly with blood unpredictable effects.

Run the film in reverse. Back to the center. Room. Clothes come off warm floor yes solid vast, back flat, buttocks soft against the wood. White ceiling familiar. Foot flat against the second mirror now both feet. From this angle a vision between long pale legs tunnel to soft black depth. Blurry tension vague angle muscles relax impenetrable all stops available.

Dressing slowly to borrow time. Curious the same street outside reflected the third mirrored wall a window. Lean out fresh air as though this side of herself reason for keeping her past. Looking up at the roof then lying in her own animation. Any background in the trade is all true. Seeing the clock more in the place. Doorway a wide cordial smile reads waiting for you to show up. Delicately walk back. Undeniable soft spot forges reason to go.

On the last wall the mirror a portrait of a young woman alone. What she sees a room with walls of leaves autumn red as though no room exists as though nature is the room. Original technique a hunch resolved by ending boundaries of self-imposed control.

Foreground opens affinity in the natural hand. "I don't mind. I'm all right now." Very decent on the warm floor making contact details recollection where the switches are. "Did anyone ever?"

Exclusive interior traps vivid color. It's different not running day and night unless you know something—an address, a wall with flowered paper. Lighting soft and scattered, but that's just talk. Eliminate the hiding places and you have all that intelligent will cut loose. She turns shifting loyalty a few degrees into the house.

# What She Then

It was this choreographed logic with no protection. She repeated herself often enough. The door rattled a fountain splashed rising pictorial memory. A half finished balance is gone. Insight through motion a cautious nomad in a trance of love kissed silent streets. Her white face turned other disturbing signs. A knife in a dark point of doing may be an exaggeration living in the present. Try to sleep. Start from scratch.

Winter sun. From this rising culture other means besides reason along a sea had passed hours with hours delicate and sensitive full of cross currents. Out of doors as no one else has ever painted it sense of purpose around a corner. His eyes, his fingers peered out to affect organs of speech dividing into parts gave them an attractiveness to begin. Words dragged so idly in order to gain human legs. Activity not doing rather than the leisure understood.

Modern cities free evidence on the opposite side. Contents of a cluttered curio window as inessential, then perplexed imagination. I sometimes got the impression she can eat alone. Do not turn. Sense the insecurity of a midnight with no pain. The runaway street fell steadily as the wall of the garden next door. Either way resolves. She waited about to enjoy a solo scene he wanted someone whose reflection laughing applied different versions of being clear and cool on the inside. Tete-a-tete in shallow water less than twenty feet away carved clocks strike the hour.

She came into the headlights covered in mud you have found some way to get inside. Combine the painful years ever since their lives fill in the picture. Stories contain early variations betray the story teller's breast no longer arms about her neck seeking comfort in the vicinity. The woman is always instinctively blending contrary and question felt the same. A favorite life is the only value out of reach. Only in twenty four hours there was time enough to let her breathe.

# Place

We know a place
where details swallow pieces
atticlike up reminiscences preserve
under hypothetical grotto
for sake of symmetry ignore



Advantage about character
privacy diagramed the agent
a species of sensible
for it would follow
we did not seek likeness thereof



As the color gold
or difference between



Mobility off center
footing a spectral retraction
down every aisle still finds
not realizing their inefficiency
their coruscation a perfect echo



Nostalgia among windmills
decay and success stand out
which thought will come next
an outline whittled and chewed
over the hedge near home

## Now Is One More

Yet sunshine
summoning all sympathy
from the middle
found its way

Chance is dense
a more appropriate ornament
inoculating direction
into sensible form
the initial solidarity
returning order
whether hunger
expresses forbidden benefits
in art or in nature

Who has not seen
rapture cleanse and penetrate
neurotic flight
wages out of context
objects of a mythologizing process

So virtuous partners
risk their all
on intellectual business
fawning tradition
bound in soft sobriety

These constant symptoms
reply in the same language
awaiting our choice
always smiling receptacles
of every shape
a talent for arrangement

On the brink
an earth dwelling sky
silently advances
fallen among myriads
stretched out on yards
to what distance
the howling evening
perpetuates night before

# The Mirror

Night surfaces from warm depth breaks silvery sleep's unconscious outside leaves tremble all of a piece against low pitched bird's call as the wind begins a gentle wave finishes on the other side of a murmured name wrought iron bed glistens with moonlight water in the basin resting at the foot of the bed makes the sound of lake lapping against the porcelain edges, no the lake sound is coming from another room something white and soft moves fast across the top of open door the man pours water over the woman's hair waterfall awkward motion as she stands water cascading her gown wet cotton gleaming white water flowing hair arms movement of hands she turns her head the room is flowing down paint and plaster raining down a fire on the dresser the mirror reflects the flames the dissolving room splashes into the floor a widening gush she parts the hair away from her face tender shining wet in the mirror over her shoulders hands clutching the white towel absorbs the light water running over the brick walls sound of rain on the windows slick streams rivers of water she gazes the mirror reflects an old woman calm eyes shawl anchored around her neck with one hand rain dripping down the reflection dropping into pools her other hand strokes against the mirror surface, a particular sound made only by the skin of a palm rubbing wet glass.

# Book Mode

*For Spencer Selby*

On the part of relief collected and remelted sets the stage. Not just the way she intended this style binding nature in different places. Change from one to two is a heavy door silently with the good sense to let her go. Estimate a schedule, on the other hand a small book proportions out of our past. It might be the irregularities, words having been counted by book buying inhabitants all over this country well versed in the merits. You as a reader receive from the author a series which has already begun. Try to talk the book. Application makes a definite page of printed feelings, allows space with the writer in the bath.

Writing and reading ways of talking to and reaching other people. Making a writing I often saw a source of community an unbroken understanding sometimes without explanation. You and I go our ways able to foretell the omissions only for a day or a little longer. Mode of the receiver on this moonlit and dream-visited planet. We feel we are certain we find ourselves believing we hardly know how or why. Habit is ten times nature minute to minute an invisible law discerning final results. Trouble lends an inhospitable ear supplicates gods bringing gifts into the sea.

Going back into the work to build up low spots in the right size and shape hold more closely together. Customary half-tone whirring outside of the book is given into hands. Anxious friends bring slight changes showing evidence to save time. Photography's delicacy of line breaking up the colors. A word here about friction whenever it can be done just a few words might save wear and tear of feelings. All this time enough professionally trained ornamental minds request unusual features. Having decided whether the book is between the lines this manuscript juggles lives before a new public. Think details, idiosyncrasies, the same size of type bound down to an art a stone and a horse gifts for a present life.

Some other means to remember plots inner parts to know correctly beforehand with regard to seasons beyond that autumn age. Then follows the period of keeping with the book. Play the part of woman the same work as women do, have connection with them but remain quiet. Anyone acquainted with design carries them at first. Similar work comes again in volumes appears verified. Printing is the adaptation of one or two signals in a general way choosing a situation. More care touches blank paper until an impression is all of your own.

# Fiona Templeton

~~~~~~~~~

is not the ladder but before we lay the ladder to the wall is the sight even not yet seen. You, perhaps, prefer the ladder's unsentimental legs or the face to the face of the wall in order to know a man's own weight or the height of a man's own body, as I may write to know the sound of a woman's own voice, or a man's. Neither knows nor wishes to know an idea not yet seen, so your telling is only tomorrow, saving your voice for the appearance I needn't hear as I ask why you can't hear that you could listen, and so, listen, my letter is addressed only after being written. Neither need the letter be read, only written, or not understood, only read, so that you can say, I read the letter, or, I tried but am unable to read the letter you wrote me. I however am able to read it, but only aloud, and only after writing it. This is why there may be an identical letter never sent, but addressed in place of a signature.

You, having completed the climb, come down the easy way, but what I must tell you is that because it is already tomorrow you open the letter, and I am sitting up on the wall, wondering whether to kick the ladder away, which wasn't there, dear, till now.

<div style="text-align:right">November 19, 90</div>

# A/Version

April 1985

for performance at Limbo Lounge, NYC,
May 15, 16, 1985
music by Elliot Sharp

for P.S.

**one**

This grip stimulates what it prevents. Pain allows nothing but itself, a holding I can't touch because in it I'm no longer myself. You deny flesh meets. This nothing allows nothing but itself.

~ ~ ~ ~ ~ ~ ~ ~ ~ ~

**two**

In the privacy I am condemned to by yours is held nothing's absence, the idea of it, which says that the idea that, the idea might be beautiful makes it, but what is there to make? *Non voglio più servir.* Use is being a cut slice of an idea with no outside edge. *Not a man who makes love to women but a man to whom women make love, he holds on to his reason for as long as he can.* You have an idea of something to be made that is not itself, but instead you have made nothing, to hold inside yourself, so hold me from knowing your inside edge. No, you have no wall. *People will be walking up to it and bruising their faces just trying to see its invisible brilliance,* You want to make an image that is not an image. I took your image for your absence. You closed your eyes at my touch, your mouth at my breath. You covered my head and your head. With torn edges you covered the heads of the images you made, then you covered the images. I can not look at the images of your head I took to cover your absence.

~ ~ ~ ~ ~ ~ ~ ~ ~ ~

**three**

A man of importance, who is neither important nor you, said that he spoke another language than our shared one, and so we could not speak. Now he makes images of walls that speak of themselves, and of knowing nothing. I have told him he will fall into caves again. This is after that, a song that is the beginning of speaking, which is not of itself, but continues because I push it with my mouth towards that not, nor desire of the not, but anything. The mouth I hold in my hand will enter where the open mouth of my breath could not, and leave again.

~ ~ ~ ~ ~ ~ ~ ~ ~ ~

**four**

I'm speaking of the jagged black edge that turns and returns, at times with an inside edge, and a wrong direction, as if I could lift the word from the page, as if I could hold its own senses that change at the touch of my mouth. This is a struggle of the will to will. Two is one word. I mean, just because, you know, time, doesn't mean that change is in one direction, that is to more change, in the sense that I've been you already. The body holds itself in a direction, which is not the direction by which the face is seen, nor how you feel about it. *But the fire of earthly desires, once kindled, could not easily be extinguished. The Stone ignored the warning of the Immortals, and continued to importune them. "We have here another instance of Quiescence giving way to Activity and Non-Existence yielding to Existence. We shall take you for a turn in the Red Dust if you insist, but don't blame us if you do not find it to your liking".* This making is of making.

~~~~~~~~~~

**five**

To begin with, it's been a while already. Is nothing irreplaceable? *No nothing, honest.* You put something into nothing and turned nothing into something. You put nothing into something and turned the thing to nothing. I put something into nothing and everything turned to nothing. Point to what is lost. That. This is the loss. They have the same shape but mangle differently, daily. Nor is the nothing of after the nothing of before. Like that something, it didn't yet exist in the time that decided it. This deciding is not of knowing. It doesn't yet exist in the time of its making.

~~~~~~~~~~

**six**

This is the arms race. Who will get up first from which holding? Your arms hold you. You turn against. I turn away. You turn towards. I turn my arms to you. You turn away. I turn on myself, in to the heart, to hold that nothing there. Yell if it hurts, No, harder, with vacuum's armless grip, and the heart falls on itself. The body no longer knows how to move. Speech and food fail in the mouth. Fruit falls from the grip without will, and my arms wave at me, my fingers play at me. What happened? Oh, nothing.

~~~~~~~~~~

**seven**

Not that the mind no longer knows how to move the body, but that it can know nothing but the nothing inside the body. The heart is avenged on the reason that turned on the body, and against the grip it could not know.

~~~~~~~~~

**eight**

Through what must nothing pass to its equal and opposite? Through what, that is not itself something (and there is no thing)? It can be no meeting, for there the two must destroy each other. Yet what is neither nothing nor something but their opposite? What something is nothing not? If I confuse myself in the profile of desire, I am not meeting in the desired confusion of faces. We did not yet exist in the time of our meeting. Nothing, that is to come, exists now.

~~~~~~~~~

**nine**

Ask out. Ask in. Not what, what for. The hardware leading the hardware dance. Appear in place of what's meant is meant. The cave is dug to trace the tree. The song is tongue. The judge is old. The song is tongue and breaks the chandelier. Not why.

~~~~~~~~~

**ten**

Finding the way up isn't finding where up is. Or kiss it from the bottom, even if I could swallow it more than you want it to be yours. A breakdown is the natural way, or he may kill her, who he really is. There is no absolute will to truth, only not wanting what you don't want meets not wanting to want what you want, down there, the same not. The glass is unmade of no earth. I am jealous of their dirty movie. This room too is closing, you in or you out. Cut it out. I look in and my speech becomes bubbles that rise to that surface and burst.

~~~~~~~~~

**eleven**

Never held each in anger either, not nothing else to say. Never is not over, only its doing, its I never ate your cake, it made me sick anyway, down from the window of the heart's shaft, with a forgetting in, not out, so never let go, touches ground's cheek as an absent argument. Absence argued is not whole. Ask out. Ask in and the furniture has moved. Give with the right hand and take with the left heart. Knowing the words will want the head to turn, and beside the story we see rising all the derision the body can fling. Yes. Stretch the inchtape and fire from the hand anything, losing the numbers too. You hadn't before noticed the surprise as the hollow moved, right in front of someone else for whom only the game moves, because playing knows why, or makes why up after because. Held up on an arrow and stripped to rank's colour, how can this be touching the arrow's shaft when you know you travel the other way, light.

~~~~~~~~~~

**twelve**

The song is dumb, the painting hung in other rooms so hounds appear geraniums if questions only say the answers. What is to be taken down if breakers love the promenade whose reason there they are but breast in two refusals to be one? Lookout viewpoints rotate in the foam's eye. Answers answer any questions and forget, tongue torn from turning the title behind the canvas, to a return address, with love. Spectators clench their hearts for him to win for them who can't, but pay, and now the T.V. shouts commercial breaks at bookshelves closed as skin that dreams it slaps love timed to reason. Americans subtract the number chosen first if equal means same in this language that also says shape and correct, and argument suspect where viewpoints have reached to a crossing passed through to abandon. Hamburger, hamburger, hamburger, hamburger, hamburger, hamburger, hot dog. Grey morning finds it harder to find the body than night's mind's eye's hard body.

~~~~~~~~~~

**thirteen**

I breathe you every day. I shit you. This is not strawberry. This is not cucumber. I am not your table. I am not your chair. I am not your bed. I am not your light bulb. This is shit. This is oxygen. This is gold. You probably can't lift what I'm falling about, and that's your floor. You shirt me up and coat down with me in your talks, on your understand, understand or imagine. There's a man there but we don't care but we don't strip. You want to salivate into my ear. I want your saliva to fall in my mouth. I swallow as we turn my head and your spit runs across my cheek to foam in my ear and you come. I can't be angry in front of him so take you out but my feeble fists just reach your chest. A train pulls in. A poster says that Spanish honey is best. I remember it running from pots, have you? and it's true.

~ ~ ~ ~ ~ ~ ~ ~ ~ ~

**fourteen**

Not, the thing deserves life, but if not the thing then trying is not nothing. Nothing means anything, but anything can be something, so get shown the door. You showed me pictures. You showed me the subject of each. You showed me laughs. So I've a new ditty that you can join in. As usual, guys, the only words are, "matter, matter". Leave your caress on the door. It allows the garden as the garden allows the room. No wrong door! Then how do they get in? They squeeze through the little holes the mind can not prevent. No wrong door! Then how do they get out? Is it not the heart on the homemade swing that ignores the wall with a shout of thief so the thief is born as one becomes two when the swing breaks and the eye and why and want and know? The heart is breath and not a picture. Send care packages but we hate baby food. Care rage happens bodies leaning ground mind we bang rave they haha haha haha haha haha ha boohoo. I'm standing there and it disappears because it's true, because it's held out.

# Steven Forth
from *Material Space*

## /*porcelain*

cleaning rag, the kitchen bathroom
with its sink of flowers,
flowering remains. not asking have
the sunshine window framed by
yellow, pigments in the water's
fragrance. staining the eye quick.

the house whole, rain window
sills white; air rubbed whole
in the cold. our hands
chafing, rubbed with vaseline, a
glossy film on water, smears,
adhering to the petals, porcelain.

wiping lint grease from the
floor, eroded tiles clean, a
shaven face. water evaporates leaving
the glass dry, the mirror
open, endless overcast infiltrates the
rooms. wiping our skin clean.


## // *ivory*

happy smile plays flute.
trimmed, hearing ivory in
its edge, a trifle
touching.
       vain in loving,
virtuous, a virile trap.

we give grateful, hungry,
sharing the other's throat.
eliding the difference, swallow
fricative burred liquids,

soft palate absorbing the queered
lemon tasting high sound.

held hands, held heads,
and necks stretched thin.
a damaged voice, paper
smooth, fluttering, the flute
notes rapid under breath.

## /// *amber*

scotch bled————a tooth
dull amber in its
ache, preserved in fluid
like old glass. remembers

apple, and creak of
ice water, the crushing
pressure of the bone.

so delicate the tongue
is loath to probe
along the gum, unhinge
and drink another tumbler.

## *IV narrowing*

allowed to continue, a natural stop in the throat's pitch, a
corded ring, tightening, that whistles where the shape is thin.
muscle spindles stretched, forced air irritates the throat with
dust inhaled and coughing briefly, emphasis or indication of
impatience.

dry carries. distinct. kept to a shape the hissing underneath
wrung white. ground. the leveling continuous, whistling eats the
silence.

an edge is noise, subsists between the interval, to calm. the air's
calm forced, each vocal wakening a need to speak, within
coherence.

## *V shore*

line breaking at the rippled edge, ebb and strewn along the shell line's questioning. written in the sand-to-water flatness, collecting fragments. the brighter colors in commotion. turbulence sorts shells by weight and surface, lines as tide recedes, laid along the contours. then edges up the beach, gathering higher, the rim awareness sea will blur with sand.

## *VI boundary layer*

continuous movement ruptured by the friction of its surface tensions, the muscle rapture spasms as our skin adheres. water pearls on fat, films, the sheen evaporating. dries as boundary layers dissolve. dry heat and mucus flares. the viscous boundaries gel, irritant, exposed to air.

## *VII*

plural a confusion
in one flock,
flight. is abandoning

altitude, at rest
innumerable differences prevail.
startle & evade.

is to vanish
part of the
world, its seeming.

## *VIII stain*

aluminum pit, aloe
a purgative, allow.
loess accumulating
fill for static.

dry river, mordant
holds the dye
fast, insoluble
ash as litter.

sputtering clean to
heat or current
passes cooling
resistance. forgiving forget.

burned for scent
slow oxidation whitening
the metal resists
refractory, absorbing airs.

## *IX*

exempt sustain, the
interval transparent
decays. idle
gracing an attempt.

equal weighted, the
hum eating softness,
filtered soft and
porous, a ceramic's

permitivity higher than
the air's. is
kept intact, a
static saturation.

## X

stress creak fills with pitch,
muting the damage. at higher
elevations density absorbs the growth;
sound falls off into an
always immediate distance. lost hours

every day is full. edging
into the dark. a year contained
by cold's effort, trying to
speak. this futile attribution of
a sound is not silence.

## XI

cold tightened growth
rings a higher
pitch, close grained,

eliminating moisture from
the wood, a vertical
imperative delayed.

capacitance enhanced by
shorter days, alignments
the frost ruptures,

repeated intervals ascending
a logarithmic scale.
an interval reduced.

the year closed.
frost hardened,
wood splits clean.

## XII

eliminate debris, the cost
escalates, indifferent to the
time allowed. to retract

an existence denied, is
claimed as part of
the common. externality.

put outside to waste.
a shared expense, depleting
a need prevails.

## *XIII*

mine an attempt, tunnelling,
the means exist until
exhausted, and walls slip.
air yellowing, expelled from

lungs shrink, wrapped in
black belonging. the tailings
end useless in pools,
slowly burning the groundwater.

 are possessed, owning the
substrate, responsible for
another use. concentration
degraded, eroding the slope.

## *XIV*

a litmus burn the creek
random burrows in its slope.
valley deepening its sides slide
closer. more intimate in the
rain. different exposures obsess a
need for control. a delay

the rain makes immediate. filtered,
soil's imprecise smooth space drawing

capillary flows. its surfaces a
volume take on weight, collapsing
fill, dimensions collapse into a
direction under. opening the slope
consumes itself, buries its potential.

## XV

decay the condensation
quiet, a flaw
in air's static
growing crystal. each
imperfect repetition blank.

## XVI

a perfect solvent's infinite
dispersal shared, cannot
be known, eliminating doubt.

what is will not
complete, preference seeking
a lower potential rest.

## XVII

Rust's slow burn releasing currents the edge bleeds into a
ground. Each shock tiny and abrupt. A precise freedom. A
reduction in exchange. The metal's electric softness blurs the
film, absorbing random flux, and stripped of free electrons is
inert. Dry longing. Nothing given to air is kept. Or wants to be.
The solution absolved is shared, our weakness vain.

## XVIII *The Large Glass*

laundered air's dust damp
chill in the glass
clings to the hum.

breeding infiltrates the cracks,
the ion swarms uneasy
equilibrium, sensitive to touch.

a ground to drain
uncertainty, the line's crazing
infinite confine.

## *XIX*

gift wrapping the
fine dry powder's
permission to ignite.
empty between points
the flash connects,
any present could

explode in the
past. a gift
of no particular
value, no determined
use. I choose
a plain paper.

## XX

edge crumbling flame
around the circle
stifled. breath consuming
what's exhaled, aware
of smaller intervals,
goes out. absorbed
into its own
refuse. healing our
dependencies claim us

*infrathin*




an empty glass of water

# Norman Fischer

## Not to Be Found

The arbitrary mindless
Persistence of objects ready to
Explode so crowded into themselves
They wait wait vainly for their masks
To coincide with an earnestness
Folded into prescience
Not to be found in words

## SIX MEN FACING A WALL OF WATER

Alarm and fatigue. People walking along shore. Sun shines, gulls and pelicans. Hoping later on she'll, no not, that any utterly thinking, so will, not. Should note. That's positive, should do that. Will pick up pack or be gone there. This spot won't hold my clothes. One more means. To think to do what's right, again the words come up into it. You'd stop, opposed, again sigh. That the various people peopled that place. Tall buildings functioned as monuments there. There was nothing funny about it there. How it was so that it made us think. We did. You came to visit us. Years ago we were close but that was years ago. Our brow an arch of half a bridge. The words like lions, kings, sitting, that state, to be also where we are. Now and then, cascade of light lights us. From an early age undone. Just a jutting out of the rug to be some shape. There is always some shape. Ever the pear there. My book is square. I lean toward you so that you prop up. Properly. Means to own that. Property. Exactly like the waves. To return to that. Everything just looks so fine on the beach. Flames shooting out of their heads. Airs, noses, raising an arm to point off at a distance. But beneath this spread of culture the old customs still remained. I took a break from this book to read that book. A lot of people talk about experience. How about that. Me, I just hobble along in a hundred clumsy ways, a thousand klutzy stumblings, pokings at the truth. Truth for breakfast. Eat, sleep, speak. And then some. Carry a camera, here, by tide's light, set on sand. Older and older so lighter and lighter. Less beams, more merry. This would suggest that. This way of doing it, later on, more of it. Words make shapes early or late. A last wave, what would be a last wave, where end wave before new wave or piece, part of wave ever. None ever. My how clever you would be there.

The words talk to each other and draw each other out. We do what we do to do, to go, to be to each what every is or would be. A temporary contradiction, a fiction. I want the door to be glass. It takes more cleaning. But it slides. It sticks often. It pokes through the screen that gives onto big paper expanse of subject matter. I just wrote it all out, just like that, this, and then this. The text can be performed operations on, hacks we are all on, then in or to it, by it, as agents of it, or it acts on us. The things would be equally real. You see, you reach out, but you annoy every one. They can't be with you because they think they are going to save you. No one but them is going to know how to be so understanding and by their deep lovingness and understanding, their givingness and openness, they are going to soothe you and salve you and save you. But no. You are going to want them to help you but you are going to go into the precise dream images, into the media. There you will find the perfectly rendered wooden image that will be you. Life is shade light and shadow. Sensitive fingertips and blood red dawns. So you'll fire up or it's a ploy. Another way to endanger the very elements periodically there is a sale. There is no real sense to this, in which it, like grease, it goes down to, then up, and it has a connection to. A lamb bone would be intellect. A lump of dough the true heart. This bird stalking by the spirit and the way and the salvation.

## II

Not a paper
your life
a thing—not

The fan's part
yet one by word
and out

Then OK
this way
to do so

haven't done
a day's work
what one counts

one knows
they seemed
to the waters

honored to read
labored there
or missed where

you came in
and cared
so pondered

a reversal of feeling
or air glazed
bits—and so

a toehold, an heir,
scion never scorned
this would be the six the night

## III

    Alarm and fatigue. You suggest a detailed scheme, a paper shore a proper chair. Sun shines, so meanings. To never do but be, be well, go away, pleasure's sense, a way, out of there. Should note. That's positive. A thing, the waters, we would share, love, and that draws it to us, originally reaching out for the nearest words to grab hold of. Does one condition the other? Does tone take precedence over precision? Does the case break ever before the mechanism warms up? And we could go on still further in this vein. Writing gets more serious as we go along. She lifted the veil, her face bloodied from the mash his punch made of it. The detective peered through the half opened window without seeming to. A square, in Moscow. Pitted again, or in. Tinkling piano, delicately clinking glasses, murmurs, perfume. There is great efficacy in community. You have to cover yourself, over, there, and so you ponder the snow, seeming substance, and wish it, pushing yourself further. Now and then; cascade of light lights us. From an early age undone, bricked, as it were, shut, because being opened so exposed, exhausting. That time would pass and thus. A matter of the delicacy of words, the exactitude. Talking about it just the jutting out of a rug to be some shape. But there is always some shape whether we shape shape or shape shapes it. If shape shapes it no property properly assuaged spreads culture, no book to read, to read that book, flames shooting out of their heads. No quiet person to be there, here, with or against, to press against your body, by the weight of it making it as if it were an article, THE person, A person, or THIS person. Eat, sleep, speak. Pour heart out. Change again. Next time there hands, arms, face, very self, attitude, habitual pattern. No USE. Carry a camera, here, by the dawn's early light, hail a cab, charge forward as the bombs burst in air, gives proof through the night that you are there, on sandy shore, laterally, lighter and lighter, in the sports arena. This is satire. That's the way to do it. These simple insistent instances of a light, there always, the one full moon, famous bridge, older and older etc. I would think out a plan. Next the dirt would fan out around a cone. The quality of the experience would guard against any indeterminate valences, the words would talk to each other, conspiring against me, as often occurs. Slope of hill out window, deer's antlers rattling dry twiggy bushes, at least that's a fixed point, no? That one is here would suggest that. The sentences don't connect and seem moreover to bear no relation to one another, this way of doing it, later on more of it. Her teeth seemed to be slowly rotting, some sort of bone disease, and perhaps that is at the root of her difficulty. None ever so clever there. Put it down, whatever it is, it's got to be, your memory, who would ever care. That it struck you that way. That it was particular to your particular life, like drawing water in a bucket out of a stream. Pen slides, wants door to be glass. But it isn't. You open it, shoulder to. But I'm doing it, you're doing it, not that we have to talk about it but we just WEAR our pants yet can't avoid seeing that they are there. You see, you reach out, touch world, can't be otherwise, things done never to be undone, each thought an irreversible depth charge, light and shadow, over and over. Each moment builds on another, you may re-write I can't re-write this but each word in sequence never deleted never goes away, periodically there is a sale it has a connection to connections every which way. There is an intellect someplace there. Someone is thinking, speaking, taking the time to make it. Softly weeping.

## IV

Each one
every thought
of something

Each vision
every vision
of something

The mind
never fixed
on nothing at all

only outside,
the part that's
always deleted

outside the story of
people we are
is to be recognized

as such, being
of the floor the grass
has become particularized

curiously indeterminate,
powerless to effect
any which way

one's self or another
like taking a drink
out of a stream

as though it were
a serum
would cure all ills

which we would
consult
like an oracle

Coming home, crossing
with ourselves
an embankment

to us, to take world
in, missing it,
nursing it along

accepting it for
what it is
apart from how

use it, lose it
make it over, win
it or break up

over it, it must
be there waiting
on other side

of thought, of
vision, one
really relevant

unadumbrated—
not even—
place there is

none to call it
or even go to
beyond the calling

only, that you
too criss-
crossed in light

are there just
as simply as

# V

Make haste to do what is good; keep your mind away from evil. Water coming in, sun low, sleep now. Do enlarge on that, make of it appeasement, a conundrum there. The sand between toes, a lark, like an altar there, in air. A man may find pleasure in evil as long as his evil has not given fruit; but when it fruits he runs from there like his hair's afire. Douses in ocean sand and wind. So what if where coming home you lose that clumsy ways, a thousand klutzy stumblings. Love what is good as if bumping into furniture. So the light, and it burns too, nor get too close to touch, nor far away to freeze. It would make us think. And so, to know what to do. Gather it little by little. At outset of day, that blush, as it first would come, and peaceful calm, set on sand. Yet there is always some shape. It is subject matter, and it comes on consecutively, first talking about one thing, then another. But we return there again and again, like a gorgeous woman. The words talk to each other and draw each other's part. Let a man avoid the dangers of evil even as a merchant carrying much wealth, but with a small escort, avoids the dangers of the road, or a man avoids drinking poison. Let him not be afraid of what is good, afraid of what looks like evil, or the ideas in his head. He picks up the white kerchief from the sand in the twilight and calls it blue. I want the door to be glass. Concepts go all a-smash. But it's all concepts! It slides better but sticks more often, giving out onto lovely expanse of equanimity. The author loitering in the rain. That would be equally real. The text so, and forward, the technologies perform what your resistances deplore. I can work with that. It will be the cone, that it's so, and you would hand her the umbrella very clearly near the park, but they want the thing defined apodictically as possible, locked, fused, anodyne. Searching time throughout for the key. I will ignore the day to day. I will never use words like television, Brillo, Kool-Aid. The guy sitting across from you at dinner has AIDS. This is not a lurid newspaper account or a shocking word in a literary text. It occasions a response. The guy sitting across the table from you at dinner has AIDS. He looks thinner than you remember him. The allure of the abutment, a dish, now this, a consequence. No one knows the web of views, how they lead here, and so produce today. Waves break in the cold in the dark the heart breaks. A wearying of force turning, the stems all crunched together, heard. At the point, around the bend, the words attractive, allure, you read on, but they will not take you away from yourself. They refuse. You are often amazed at your own cleverness. You notice—exactly now—you've lost awareness of your body, that you're sitting on a chair, that you are yourself reading. There is no sense to this the confusion that you are writing the text, it goes down to, then up, and it has a connection to. Who's to say the limit of a skull? We stop when the plot's all done. Neither in the sky, nor deep in the ocean, nor in a mountain cave, nor anywhere, can a man be free from the power of death.

## VI

and we will not
call it by name

so tame it walk
away or release

so a course set
any harm meant works

here, that power attends
in the force of it

the dull urge pulls
who cares to come

against the water's lip
would wash there adrift

# Gil Ott

from *The Whole Note*

## Fourth Fourth

Moving, variant ornithography of those uninitiated

made into memory by the me briefly incarnate. Full of myself on successive nights dense and alone sings

you back. Need keeps the book of dying open, the language common after all. Relieved, the task finally changing prompts tapping my reserve

feeling, now, wise to its edge. Where are you risk any detail of what's in me, having been tricked by the image of a man. Softly pain the intuit

applications under authority of breathing. I drive this one, I get winded

calendar's familiar, speed and abruption.

Of one's existence, adopted to debility to have it out of silage steeping, inescapable. Onto one woman

another inequity hoped to thirty to settle. Cripple, for the platen his chest opened, the emote standing in phials reminiscent

indomitable due free movement among bodies, that waits and will absorb that's dished. Christian to these passions

without time this time the visitor will burn along forced choice of hosts. Virtue to heat, crumble, pass as the village forgets

he still walks unassisted. Minded the story of a life he'd got foot on, so careful.

In the round of abnegate scoring among locking peer workers, demands and their deceptions, love made

torn, at times, out of wallcovering, animated to destroy my own house. As from a wallet, applied simile fond, a sense of mission. Sincerer kin cop to my survival in secrets. Hell sounds

capable over a pit losing everything. Gentle evolved

self of absolutes absolute congruence this then repeated discovery. Wake to me aisle between waking us simultaneously. A slot for putting worry came to pray

with effort out of a role. Foretold the under this chair I sit on, humbled and green, and gray.

Descend, or overturn a temporary order for a cold one. An opening is in or out testing the condition run

my skin off, free of constraint. Blind me at speeds my legs toward enduring. Of my antithesis

scrawl wasting who said patiently absorbing? Scrabble in any direction glory little, like a squirrel. Path of indifference, subtending achievement equally

opaque. Without me, you

trunk, stone, cave entire to chance and chance cohesion of mind. The warrant at dark, and that early.

And the little wind ran, animating random. Sluggish, count warmth in a scrap I'm breathing the regular foam

gutter, iron to crease anger. Weight to conform all workers' surprise at the appearance of the sun. Another day. Pad flat

the curse the bit of sidewalk soaks craving liquid. Heavy, bulk, a state all interior coat over

head and feet skewed toward no meal. Dancing this way to beg me, muscle is common. Some air, that too

private decay, the eloquence of concern. Piled on every bone felt, and beside me, unexpected, me.

In whose ears the ringing ebb hid, a shadow moving on the sidewalk. Quick amid a piecemeal sea that's come to inhabit

gently by the throat. Age by age, a syllogism to the sounding bow grows deeper as the stop moves on, the interior

with difficulty to any appointment crumbles. What protected artery this weak, human circumstance advances the distance resonance marks. Today, this one end

the knees fed paste and chore. Back at centuries, bone inserted

bruise and get away, the interior recovered. Drink lesser, rested vapor.

Part by part removed, the pleasures first. How at the end the inhabitant looks on past habitation

treed, out of breath, less permanent affecting landscape than its cold lake or hill. Dark walk on

leak blood. Dispassionate grace the water's edge

reach to what hypothesis uncertainty led the spirit. Still, moving, speaking, incomprehensible. Feet set in mud, decayed, and other feet

tirelessly composed. From lap and slaver crusts tenuously amid succeeding motilities endure, some history, any. Fear, but fear's

subject unremembered, everywhere present.

Prone to the observance, a formal end only, blurred with or without
morphine decides to live. I have made a mistake, a meandering

stasis, down a notch and starting over. Someone else's surgery
pulled a knot out, left a man handled roughly

bumped and thrown what dirt brackets. Possessed of this violence,
a plea remains. Fed on seed here, a small black bird

far and still admissible. I will build a body of utterance, that fooled
me. The odor will stay, and I

will walk away.

# Steve McCaffery

## Critique of Cynical Поэсис

Comrade Krasheninnikova
I am answering your question.
      Esperanto of the cortex should
take place a little to the left
of one ear. Please ensure that all
the ur states are marked upon
the site of this difference. Moths
of the mind are traditionally
temporal, however, the sutra through
its murmur is bound to offend.

      Inform Department Ignoramus that this
is not a sentence. Is a sentence.
      We will let you know
if this is certain to the Caucasus
(nowadays the migrant apples bruise
if you remove the chestnuts)

      Which means it's tea
and time for ice which captures us
but not by much. All primary positions
being otherwise we are far more moderate
when dispossessed (though sounds i think
recede no further than our urban logic).

An age


is still a phrase loaned back
to the rim of each appeal by vicinity
so that the trick remains to preserve our we
      as a siamese connection.

No more to write now but the words
The train now standing is metonymy.

Conjectural and sediment to emendation
lets me add that it's okay for you
     to relax with the smoke from the other room
whilst we in the thought of codeine sobriety
     and with a qualitative north to the questionnaire
win all your downhill points.

# The Code of System Four

We entered a city consisting entirely of grey thursday mornings. But the verb enter seems partly inappropriate plus appropriate itself seems wrong. So it would be wrong to say the city could be entered though all its thursdays are grey and though grey itself consists entirely of its mornings. Today then is the morning when the verb to enter will seem wrong. Today as the day plus all the inappropriate parts themselves that still seem proper.

So we can leave the city alone. Plus by ourselves. And having reached another city on a day like any other day we can stop to say we can drop in on a day whose morning registers an offwhite mood entirely. Plus we can say we have entered a verb which seems wrong and wrong in the entirely correct sense of wrong. Wrong being wrong and day being day. Hence tautological. Plus inappropriate.

But a passage made entirely through a tautological gate seems proper. Proper in the tautological sense of proper plus the sky is not grey. Plus the day as the sky whenever grey appears as the mutilated memory of some other more important colour. Colour in the proper sense of colour. The gate was simply a gate in its proper sense. Plus we all went through it. Through it to where? Seemed wrong. Through of course to where we were. Where we were in its proper sense of where we were leaving.

Plus leaving for what? Leaving still to enter plus passing through it merely to have passed through it. That specific quality of sky seemed obvious plus something about a memory of asking. Asking as what? Asking in the tautological sense of asking. Plus the memory of having asked. Eventually an entry could be made through the proper use of equivalence. Equivalence in the sense of balancing those terms remembered that allow the verb to be inserted. Plus the verb to insert appeared wrong. For passing through the gate seemed the same as passing behind it. The same as equivalence.

Or sky. Sky to where? Sky to behind itself. But behind itself seemed wrong. We were actually above the ground but not entirely in the sky. Someone remembered the verb to float. Meanwhile it becomes sufficient to simply state a reference to gate and gate in some more important other sense of gate plus the need to make our entry equal. Equal to what? Equal to a balancing of the terms pass through and pass behind. Plus a special use of pass behind as pass beyond.

Plus the phrase disguised as morning in the special sense of converted to a date and time. Time as simply time. Plus time as the time it takes and more precisely as the time it took us. Took us where? Took us to a line linked to a certain colour on a different line we had to cross.

Therefore it seemed sufficient that we make our mode of entry in a simple reference to gate. Gate in the obvious sense of noun plus the gate itself within a space converted to the simple act of opening a passage through a wall. A wall to where? Plus a simple wall around. A wall around what? Plus a wall in the sense of a metaphoric act of human balancing. However balancing equally became the paradox of site of who we were and who spoke us. Plus the inserted problem of this story that we couldn't be when we assumed disguise could reproduce conversion to some other more important type of problem.

Plus the problem of what colour for the sky seemed wrong. Sky being wrong and wrong being day. Plus the paradox of time. Time as what? Time as the time we took to enter and decide the verb to enter seemed entirely wrong. Therefore our constant reference to passage and equivalence seems correct. Correct in the sense it seems correct that through the gate we were experiencing the tautological need to refer.

# The Printer to the Reader

A signal through space defines this group:

>at the foot of a hill,
>through a hole in a fence,
>from one state to one province;
>by a raft in a set.
>from this hoof to that hook.

In more radical encounters direction shifts to somewhere in the following:

>having an internal shell,
>describing a known state of things,
>suggesting a predetermined disposition,
>attacking a primary growth.

These paramount beliefs revive the following despairs:

| | |
|---|---|
| sudden seizures | graceful replies |
| maladjusted declensions | symbolized parts |
| unrecognized grandeurs | deoxidized claims |

Such analogues to instance via detour lead to neighbourhoods like these:

>hat hatch:
>prefer preferable;
>trilateral trill,
>kid kidnap:
>cub cube.

We may contrast that sequence to this set which intervenes:

| | | |
|---|---|---|
| antiphon | swivel | predicate |
| chowder | "instrument" | rodeo |
| discharge | bunt | dirigible |
| bungalow | inanity | "waistband" |

To return predictably to the following:

    somebody    somehow    somersaulted
    something    sometimes    before    someone
    solvent    somewhere    soothed

The next exploited paradigm implies a legislative sanction:

    nineteen, seventy-four, eight, twenty,
    six, nine hundred, seventeen, thirty,
    five, two, eleven, six, ten.

We move closer to a theme in the following continuum:

    action in.    arbitrary nature of.
    classification by.    differential structure of.
    nonrepressive nature of    inordinated repression by.
    structure in.    transparency of.
    victimization by.    weakness in.
    yearning for.    parallel risk within.

The assumptions in the Model lead to these displacements:

    Popeye
    Froozles
    Dennis the Menace
    Spiral Zone
    Sesame Street
    Divorce Court
    Star Trek.

In contrast the following closed thoughts signal a retreat from Being:

    pipe equals synephrine
    gyve equals twist.

The objective contradictions find resolution thus:

> when indigo then puce,
> if ochre not madder.
> neither violet nor beige,
> as purple so green.

At issue is the register which designates these sounds as sites:

> as, it,
> on, up,
> in, of,
> or, us,

The next examples fix a pathos in exterior marks as fact:

> Geneva 1793
> 342a Great Portland Street.

Their evolution as interiorities diminish in the following breaks with truth:

> cook botch spavin
> Bolshevik clinamen plus maroon.

The next intensive aggregates produce a vague suggestion of the Plot:

> Ice octoplasm.
> Reciprocality plus obligation to invade.
> Ice reticence.

None of the following exists inside the tradition we call passage:

> the act of turning over,
> the description of leaping suddenly,
> the verb to discharge;
> the complicity of driving away.

Two of the next three tactics mirror social practice not the Real:

>    I have cleaned my teeth.
>    I have read Saussure.
>    Last week i walked to Los Angeles.

The twilight turned murky as they closed the door inside the implications of the following names for where:

>    labyrinth ... highway...
>    portico... barbecue...
>    syndicate...collage...

The rules of substitution still agreed on permit the use of the following complex form:

>    A propositional affront destroys the
>    memory of change:
>
>    Spinoza as anagram.

With the nasal passage opened by reason of the lowered velum, the following phrase flows through the nasopharynx to mark the centre of this end:

>    pigeon should be pidgeon.

# Laura Moriarty

## The garden

An army massed on the border
A hat on my head
Keeps the sun from my eyes
More than one border is involved
Filled with light

And heat and water
And coffee again paradise
With quiet prepared
Mask at my side or your side

You are on my side
With time to write or
I have a shelter a sealed

Man rests by his mask
The world is thick above and around him

No time

# La Ruota

Fortune is shown in her most common form

Dreaming of rain

The words exist in the original language

She is attached to a wheel

Being entirely transformed into the act of turning

Like taste left in the mouth

She signs her name with her hands

Helpless as gravity

Finding irresistible force the object

Fortune is naked

Retrieved from a status not unlike

Any other tied thing

Or escapes like breath from the head or changes air into water or fire

And back again

A thing inside another thing There is no repetition

And yet more common than desire is

Fortune captured

## What is said

Their words can be used against them

They are faithful and confident

We are them in their sense

In ours we dance to a slow song

One example of a solution is strength

Or in numbers

Where we are multiple

The story is said to unfold

Their words to be said again

By others pretending to be us

But they are men/women and we are women/men

It's like another planet

Or like people who don't see themselves

Though they stand before each other

Their words said

What is claimed

A companion piece to what is said
If I had put it all on red
Or on black I would be a gambler
And this would be my story
But I am not that
Object if you will or if not
This is not a practice hand
What is claimed
Is that chance exists
Spinning us in or out
Time is on the side it's always on
Like a bracelet like the physical
Hand it surrounds
What is claimed

# Miniature

The manuscript suggests an allover approach to life. Instead of sky there is design. There is a consistent relationship with perspective. There is no use for it. The designs represent each other. A tree is about to become part of a seamless landscape. The background is pure. It repeats. It is blue but has no more reality than the formula for oxygen. The tree doesn't either. It was a thousand years ago but nothing has changed. You don't hear my voice when I write. I don't hear yours when you read. Representation of the body does not occur but the subject is obvious. The tree doesn't fall. Algebra is invented and then lost. Chemistry.

# We see

Twilight
Weather bad
Or here warming warning
Spring can't be
Dangerous this fast

The past mistaken
For what happened
An unimaginable scene
Accompanied by a jackal

This figure also not
Known not said
Blind sight when you

See what you can't see
Illusion or change

You can't know

## Song

There is a song
About repetition
There is a red sun
Incoming like a siren
Or the steady

All clear all wrong
That we see each other
Flatly
Long range

Life as in taking too much
Describes the weapons
The words blood

Friendly the boys
Among them fire

Us

# Physics

The bowl of fruit makes its own sun. We leave our maps behind and get into the pure distance. People tell us what we want to know. There are armies of thieves. The thing they want most. The radio is like being present. Simultaneously one sleeps. One reads a letter. The world is folded. The afternoon is almost over. Yellow apples fall onto a rug. Repetition is implied in the way things bend. We respond to the natural laws. We are lost. A tent on the plateau. Nothing to stop the wind. The bowl in slow motion appears to pour. The woman to hold the letter steady.

We get to the point of only reflected light. Your glasses ache on your face. You stare at the way roses put shadows on a vase. A drawing is made of tar, masonite and plaster. They are called black roses but they are red. Made of tile with the minerals baked in. One after the other like the white spots on dominoes. There is a reversal. She is a physicist. Her numbers represent events. Your eyes at rest in your head. Your words in your throat.

## We were

When it started
When it ended
We were there
We are uncontrollable
In our passions

The war is everything
Goes on as before
The air in my head
Is the same air

Used as thought or shot
Or song repeated
Doesn't end

We are persuaded we hear princes soldiers women
On the air fire metal water men darkness

We are there again

The meter running
While we speak
Calculates an equal
Silent figure known
To us adds to our sense
Of what is not
Impossible
To betray by speech alone
The meter the figure knows
Speech is free or almost
Free because it is not
The cost is written even
Spoken forever is owned
By each one who knows
The meter is told

# Leslie Scalapino
from the play, *The Present*

### Scene 8

(Music. In the darkness/slides, **HM** is wheeled out. Slide of the moon follows supertitle slides. The only movement once the light comes up is **W1** crying on **M1**'s shoulder. **W2** and **M2** imitate their poses.)

Slide: **THE MUSCULAR MOVEMENT**

Slide: **IS**

Slide: **COMING FROM SOME**

Slide: **BLACK ROBES**

Slide: **BLOWING WITH NO**

Slide: **EYEHOLES.**

Slide: **THAT**

Slide: **ARE OUTSIDE**

Slide: **THEM**

(Lights come up on stage, which is slide of huge moon held throughout)

**W2:** The man and the wife who's weeping, with the burning car outside them.

**W1:** He's quiet, isn't jeering, from inside movement that's in him, standing.

**W2:** The desert is outside them and the moon is.

**M1:** It's out in front of them so that it's in it.

**W2:** bright moon is in front of them.

**W2:** In the desert that's on fire, the black robes are blowing out on it

**M2:** not in the line of the spirals.

**M1:** They're going at a trajectory with no movement in them.

**W1:** (moves center) I want so much to be where I was before I was me.

(Stage action suspends)

**WWP:** Trying to be in the night as day.
       Pushed out and so is in the day when it is night.
       The moon is in front.
       It is on the plain.

(Stage action resumes)

**W1** The moon is in front of me so that there is nothing in me—
    yet on the rim the girl spits on me.
    for a flicker.

    The girl spitting on me.

(**W1** comes up to **W2,** speaking to her)

**W2:** Her being so immature that the friends stare at me creating a conformity to which if I object I'm merely self-serving.

**M2:** It is invalidated by having occurred,

**W2:** (she turns to him accusingly and says sarcastically)
    in me.

**W1:** to be what I am before I am me.

**W2:** it is pushed out in

**W1:** the moon in front,

**W2:** which is before.

(Stage action suspends)

**WWP:** rather than me.

(Stage action resumes. **W1** & **W2** slowly get angry and loud. They are responding to a former experience with others as if that is with each other. **M1** kneels and lights a candle on a carburetor lying beside the car seat.)

**W2:** The friends create this conformity which is limpid, occurring before.

**W1:** They don't have faces staring.

**W2:** Why did one see them before.

**W1:** They'd say it is self-serving to see this.

(Stage action suspends)

**WWP:** And so anticipating.

(Women breathe heavily)
    breathing in and out.
    The breath is in the moon

(Women come to life, very angry)

**W1:** that is outside

**W2:** in front:

**W1 & W2:** (they turn to the men) It isn't in me.

(**M1** kneels and blows out candle on carburetor to right of them. Moon and stage lights go out; no break in action, mood shifts during next lines)

**WWP:** So it doesn't matter if one is walking it is in the trees that are in the blue sky.

Birds go by.

So the day is in the night at once.
I felt joyful.
These events happen slowly before me.

(Stage lights fade up; men caressing women as if to console them.)

**W1:** He's holding the tips of the rib cage like fins and the member put in the end. Comes.

**W2:** (walking toward **W1** and circling back. **W2** speaks as if having the other woman's memory or commenting on it favorably:)
   Had been on it.

(Women walk away. They pace horizontally, **W2** following **W1**. **M1** has taken off the mask of James Dean.)

**M1 & M2:** it occurs in the present but before me.

**W1:** Seeing on the street the blue burnished face banged-up walking.

**W2:** I followed him, who'd been on the garbage.

**W1:** He continues walking ahead.

(Freeze)

**WWP:** Being outside is simple
   It's pushed out there.

   The tool is completely distorting, and having a feeling highlights that putting a lining under it.

(All four on stage; actors begin walking in place, facing front. Huge moon slide hangs above them. They stroll in a line but as if each are alone.)

**W1:** Walking

**M2:** and is in it.

**W2:** This lovely moon that was out there,

**M2:** in the day,

**M1:** orb

**W1:** in front of me.

**W2:** The hennaed man

**M2:** alive for only an instant,

**W2:** (turns to **M2** contradicting him)
    had never been alive—

**W1:** and so the breath is outside.
    Without the moon.

**WWP:** I—

(As if she is commanding the lights to go out, which they do)

**WWP:** I couldn't sleep and yet couldn't sit up either.
    I have to see the night but with my eyes closed, from
    being tired.

    and therefore immature.

    communal is completely simple being outside.
    only with the moon in front of me.

    Walking with no one there.

    is not doing anything.

(Her light goes out. Moon slide off)

## Scene 9

(In this scene, all elements and images are swirling together. All image slides seen previously flash before us, movement from all scenes are shown. The **stagehand** wheels **HM** around, etc.)

**WWP:** (in darkness) What One Sees Inside:

**W1:** It is moving backwards or turned around.

(**W2** sees **HM** wheeled around by **stagehand**)

**W2:** (astonished) The hennaed man

**M2:** alive for only an instant,

**W2:** (to **M2**) who's never been alive

**W1:** is it.

**WWP:** and not being myself riding up the street a while ago,

**W1:** (walks to right) people coming out or standing. Crossing, and they're alive for an instant

**W2:** (walking to left and sandbox) the same as the hennaed man.

**WWP:** *(as which is in this)*

**W1:** and so it's in them.

**M1:** who may see each other.

**W1:** There isn't minute movement.

**M1 & W1:** Not breathing

**W2:** and then the bursting straight trees with their leaves.

**W1:** It is eliminated from this.

(**W1** & **M1** return to car seat where **M1** lies down on **W1**, then rises)

**WWP:** The grasshopper is invisible, and the man puts his member into it. Turning it around, in the dark that's in the part of the day that's light.

**W1:** Seeing the man with the burnished face

**M1:** which is not anguished and which is

**M2:** from the shiners

**W2:** who'd been lying on garbage

(**M1** & **W1** kneel and bow)

**M2:** is

**W1:** not while sleeping.

**W1 & W2:** He's a mature being.

**WWP:** One can see during the day.

**W2:** The grasshopper is invisible in the day, and he puts his member into it.
    It comes in the relaxed gel.

**W1:** (comes forward, center) There isn't that day.

## PART II - The Present

### Scene 1

(There is no pause or break except music and instant of darkness. **W3** stands up and interrupts as if a heckler talking from the audience, with detective novel in hand. **WWP** in her own world. Stage dark but being cleared by the actors who go back and forth. **W2** pushes a broom. **W1** is heard from the darkness.)

**W3:** Why the form of the detective novel as if it were a certain thing known which is about finding corpses.

**WWP:** it is out before. (as if answering her objection)

**W3:** Seeing *(our)* actual in reality dying in that the *(other)* finds the corpses after they're dead.
    Other reflects only him, which is why he is
    isolated.

(**WWP** makes a small noise, disagreeing or reacting. **W3**'s voice is proud, argumentative)
    Bob doesn't like it when

**W1:** (standing untying her shoe, leaning against right wall, finishes **W3**'s sentence responding to her)
    it is lovely

**W3:** as being convention.

**WWP:** Or if there's suffering.

**W3:** Convention can be made without suffering.
    It appears to be convention only and

**W1:** (she is smiling, still untying her shoe addressing **W3**)
    is lovely.

**W3:** The fake canned sense of happiness we're supposed to have in our culture, which isolates one, is not the same as the

**W1:** (it is as if she's contradicting her) lovely

**W3:** images.
    A *book* is calm because it is serial. which is

**WWP:** a form unrelated to suffering.

**W3:** (opening book)
>The black gardenia in the mouth of the running
>dog is the inner man. it seems. as it is (she
>indicates the stage and actors) shallow, which
>is this loop.

(Blackout. **Slide:** "The Present" title and author again with music, as if the play is just starting now. It is held in silence as they're clearing the stage.)

### Scene 2

(Lights up revealing stage being cleared. **W3** again gets up but this time moves onto stage.)

**W3:** she moves her hands creating a line in the air, using the detective novel to suggest this imaginary line. Her tone is light.)
>Realism:
>Moving in a real terrain that is thought of as
simply itself, having no shape or view given to it. a city. so if one is in that can see it.
>the viewer is in the center of it, moving. beggars. cars. Someone comes by. It is an actual historical event though with a wide loop that separates one from it
>It is so that one is a mannerism in the terrain
which is simply itself.

**W2:** (as she leaves the stage indicates a blue pool that is painted on the floor, as if agreeing with **W3**):
>The intense blue water on the desert with cattle
coming to it.

**W3:** The loop is there...
>that the nature as such of the person is romantic is given as such if it is. in the same place.

**WWP:** people's suffering or such,

**W3:** there is the loop that separates from it. so that it really is close.
        the separation (for someone) isn't being alienated.

(**M2** passes by and snatches detective novel from **W3**'s hands, removing 'prop' as part of clearing stage)

(Blackout. **Slide**, which is hand-drawn in color:
        It is so that one is a mannerism in the terrain
        which is simply itself. The intense blue water
        on the desert with cattle coming to it. The loop is there.

---

        There is a similarity to our innocent provincial nature.
        That enabled the war recently.)

### Scene 3 - "Reading" Scene

**Slide** of a motel at night with a neon sign saying "Motel" and a long car parked in front of it. **W1** & **W3** sit in lawn chairs in casual pants or shorts. **W1** reads detective novel. **W3** with newspaper. Motel slide is held in light so it's faintly visible.

**WWP:** This is the present time in that it is inner.

**W1:** There is a similarity to our innocent, provincial nature.

(**W3** says last three words of **W1**'s at the same time)

**W3:** That enabled the war recently. There are the individuals but they are

**W1:** simple and innocent.?

**W3:** (filling out the thought, as if to explain herself to **W1**)
        Qualified, relative, not centralized.

**WWP:** It is before the area of apprehension, or behind it or alongside.

**W3:** The center is empty.

**WWP:** Everything is always present-time.

**W3:** therefore there is no content.

**WWP:** there is no present.

**W3:** (she is holding the detective novel and speaking about it)
    One doesn't see there's a center or that it's empty until later or ever know where this occurred.
    One has to *read* the whole thing, of the various parts in it to know this.
    Being past the center of each of the various parts later: the events of the pulp or detective novel/B movie meet and *are* our culture.
    The latter exists less than the life.

**W1:** (playfully attempts to snatch the novel in the air from **W3**, who snatches it away)
    They simply go out, where they find corpses; and come back home again.
    That's the only action.

**W3:** so there's no 'life', really no distance between it.
    in that space has been compressed. conventional/ supposed 'actual' life has been eliminated that is content so one is calm. one is in it and it is still.
    Other cannot reflect only him; he cannot be isolated, in the form.
    The detective novel/B movie is a copy like a xerox;

**W1:** (smiling, as if making a discovery)
    that is why it is so beautiful.

**(W1 & W3** freeze)

**WWP:** In the Midwest, there is no other. A line
    is separate, this is the only life there is.

(**W3** leaves chair and comes forward, draws a line at the word "line" in space while announcing:)
>isolation

**W1:** (trying to catch up in thought as if anticipating and questioning)
>other reflects only him, which is why he is isolated.?

**W3:** (sweetly condescending, referring to **W1**)
>The child has no sense of the flowering bum.

**WWP:** then suffering isn't anything as it's oneself.
>The Midwest is nothing *but* suffering.

**W3:** (in response to **WWP**)
>That speaking is a copy supposedly of life, which it resembles not at all, or of others and inner and historical events at the same time is its actual present-time.

---

(Blackout. **Slide** of hand-drawn text and blue square of sky:
>In the Midwest, there is no other. A line is separate, this is the only life there is.

>>isolation

>Other reflects only him, which is why he is isolated.
>The child has no sense of the flowering bum. then suffering isn't anything as it's oneself.
>The Midwest is nothing but suffering.)

# Margy Sloan
from *On Method*


Roughly comparable in itinerant classes, as animals we were given
to curiosity. Where are we now?
To doing something, we appeal
notion by notion within a sample space,

a litter of features. Since we ask, they are
devoted (reclusive) to our senses. The stylus drags
prevailing views: winds through waves keeping
track, counting is counting as. In future research,
seas spot sun, a chimerical experiment

the rules will bend. The bind is you, in a word,
a gesture, peripheral aspect of proliferation, migration
along the horizontal axis (world appears center screen):
out left nothing out right.



Air or a set: idea's lifespan. Start here:
count crowds clouds flood. Nonentities
populate thickly and solidly as we sweep away
the grounds, fantasia categories. Let, for convenience,

the data, however doubtful, speak for itself. Writing up a storm
the stylus wears away the perimeter; leaving it
out left nothing. Out right fictions assume
prevailing views. Winds through waves keeping
the contours in shape, gradients blue

melt in a deformable mirror; the palace loses a wing
in an elapse. Ground to shape gathering starlight, here
is a place perennially estranged, previous to current,
literally present in the midst of the most remote mixups.

In the place above mentioned matter of making
clear first meditations, a hill is the mark a wave possesses
just as a solution
to retreat. A hand needs a guide in ruling a line, cancelling
out. Left nothing right. Assume within

eye to eye contact there will be gradations of a sky
and a range in that universe of indefinite recursions
within within, withal. Dark, light, there, here,
hold on. As we circle our question, trying to make
straight for its heart, orders of prediction dissolve in the ratio
of our advances. Where are we now?

Where was I?     Falling into paralogical
esthesia; the great instrument by which
certainty has been given to precedents is a volley of pleas.




The facts, in a flood, are twisted; imbricate clutter:
    fate, property or
right? Assume nothing within this tiny device,
a line of defense straight ahead, conceptually
    straightforward.
A simple declarative sentence has its sound
seeking guidelines (ornate, palatial),
solve for excess; here are we.

The reflection of our or both is less than unity,
a just  solution,
it's a wash, for shaping the future. Restless techniques
console us with passing notions; before is a heap
of remnant forests, after is a field
of furious winds. Bluish, glassy,
melting in imaginary numbers' retreat,

the succession of negative vistas runs; in the following expression,
the guide's expression is fantastic, stopped with a look.

The principle of least time disputes answers apparently
within reach. Assume the path of a right angle, nothing
in the way. Now listen.
Sound comes from everywhere, here for instance. The
  other aspects
of nature—birds, flowers, rocks, and trees—
are details in the system, celestial
unfortunates. Also, walls will shed.
With the most ancient device

to rule our sleeping selves where notions are our
guide, lines seeking
to follow their path must make the time
of passage most. Is sorting stars
a solution at odds
with those experienced when we're awake, yet as
  solitary and as retired
as we are if seen from a hot star? Good, better, best: the degree
of the angle as you slice it depends on the ratio
of space corresponding to the time

it takes for one part of speech, its music
to cross-fade into another.




Sine curves flutter as a span collapses, a sight nearly
within reach. From this remote spot, we will, we must, assume
  there was a close call.
Now listen: off the foaming peaks, sound goes everywhere, even

flying to other aspects of nature—beds, bolts, sleep and sighs—as details
in the system, celestial litter. Textbook beams
of light take the path of least time till hitting a wall.
Every time we look up, a trail of forms
is trying to cross the desert sands. We, finding
our guide, formerly lost but
unmissed, by means of losing track of the coordinates,

got mixed up. The Milky Way is a suspension
or a nebulous solution scattering light, stellar winds
unheard; as its signs of life, or among them,
never distinct from the body, we can never
leave to have a look. No, not really. Our powers are bent
on fixing the machinery, burnt
bearings, frozen works. Weary means thread
the branches; at a prefixed threshold, unheard by some,
acoustics sacrifice appearances, slide the bolt,
a tension span, an

ancient device, at most.

And so: primary colors and all their issue convene, continue,
    sine die, falling as a

shower on plains within a flyover range, assume such names as
    they fall, though as many unseen, most unnamed, thus
winding up a line of inquiry. Boundaries created by schisms
in climate and attitude fly in the face of convenience. Air power
    pushes
divisions around, but even as attention to a long day's
expectations put to rest in an alien bed, just as restful
as unfamiliar, unsaturated with associations, there among the
    desert's
speechless creatures going through formalities, saying, in effect,

try this, factors of response die down. It's night.
But is it dark? All the same, the dreamy
track of (un)missed coordinates means the losing of or hold
on the mind of blue sands, red sands, glitter
flickers through transparent grains
of colors never mentioned
in a renowned guidebook to the interior:
the lights were out. Issue of writ
of habeus corpus; you should
have the body, why not? A white
pill for day, blue for night; the present
system envisions a response time

not the same as the intended
expression falls apart, declined.

Night-life is quiet. Cross-referencing to the future perfect,

vast new forms of certainty are predicted. Could it be supposed
    that there was no world, nor any place where the very same
    thoughts of the sleeping are seen as blanks,
a soundtrack of missed notes. Or losing coordinates the means
or the mode, that is, wherein disputes resolve into a touchy subject;

a light goes on in a science of reflections
which corrupt speech; another red, cloud, may call

attention to the wing from here, its metal skin and bolts.
A block of sky stretches away neither black nor a blank
of unlike appearances. All in favor intended to
say, why, what's been crossed with sound building codes behind
    that slashing roar?
Subjects dear to the heart rule
out foreclosure, but in the case of fire
rush to the imperative. Crackles in the branches bloom, bolt starward;
a meandering tour of the remaining trees must be a second-
    hand event
in an architecture of acoustics; the walls are rushing enclosures
    twisting baffles.

Eye witness accounts, though intelligible, will have been muddied

by anecdotal engineering. Across an expanded field of vision
endoscopic procedures demand that hand and eye find each
    other all over again.




As day returns, sands twist and dray heavy starlight in.

Observe the sand to the left, to the right. A palace will be
    appearing up ahead. There, all the known indices are stored,
    past, present, future. An index of kinds will be embedded
    near the end. Do not be afraid of being

unmissed. Losing ground leaves a faultless track. Disputes will
 be animated,
will have been traversed as soon as a judgement arrives.
The guide, making an impression of warmth, is waving. So read

dear subjects, rule the heart

out of the picture
where each picture is composite, each is the same but the one
 with the flaw
speculation in the works
makes hard to find. Stay right where you are; illumination
will do the moving. Dark is never dark enough
to hide all. This paper outlines the steps. A comparative study
 highlights each trip with graphic equivalents. Put your hand
 out. Sound rooms are very small, aren't they?
In its precision, a magnetic dip at plain's horizon will attempt to
favor all running off in unlike directions. If intended,
there will be many choices, all good. Saying we, we're
 not sure; do we mean to include, exclude anyone

not us? Throngs will be rounded up to an even number; day
leaves by degrees.
A grid nets the plain lights up.

Migrant fixity impresses stream's metallic surface, a former moment,

but it feels the same as ever. One analyst might write complete
 subject on the line connecting on the horizon with dark
 clouds but another might prefer mobility, experience, petty
 crimes. Who's counting. Reviewing the forms of see, come,
 do, go and fall for thoughtless omissions amply discovering
 what is already there

to track down, put your foot down. Emotional coordinates,
   losing their colorful streak, are not a means of
speculation. Works in
progress, of kindness, cover cross purposes. Sandy, grassy, or
   housing a wood

dark is a still tract;
animation lives through it, there, there.
Where the data never do speak for themselves,
in balance, there is no reply which persuasion does not
subject to the rule of special
affection. One settles down, another sighs, this one is among an
   unknown number
fleeing, the speaker and one or more others that share in the
   action. Days are of several kinds, and as in each lagging
   slightly in some sense behind any other, attention clutters
   intention. Or in the order of meaning
reversed, within centuries, seconds pile up in friction between
   suface
and interior. At the edge, appearances' unintended
side effect, likeness will cloud
any blue: metal blue, gadget blue. For the sake of
what idea, reticence to qualify—had listened, would
have, will,—included in a trail of primes any one

so dear to any other one wandering in a countless predicament.

# Melanie Neilson

## Disfigured Text #2

Presences to throw, etc.
Steve Sax sez: Hind is set aside for thur temple saying
click, urban provincial people had sharp spec.
Your elected official t-t-shirts up the or
off their heads and they don't grow special meanings shot
special words harp specific word. Sonam to death,
sun, cloud one hundred times.
There was a steep cancer disfigurement, exercise and death.
These are cut down I open beam and stone.
And perfection cidal fog which blows in with
pet horoscope hanging succulents,
remarked that I am dot dot dot spots like sweats or sits
of light and invisible ease in French.
Joy and envy awkwards and forwards at tear back to bed.
Light and motion was called out in for the trees
around the windows.
Appear everytime headlamps are pro cho in the forest
of trees quiet sonic ts (whole trees overgrown).
The switch we. The fingers much can paper take.
Thousands of headlamps a country.
The tired the mass produced cars
ate them through practice.
A sun clear active avenue plowed from as winter approached.
Around a great warmer climate laid-off from a product.
The park is lying and being in the minutes
instinct from dream job.
Vida loca, loose press my fingers.

# Disfigured Text #3

Words, urban pro.
May I say as your elected official
not like leeks. You cut off their heads.
Of what shirts up the ghost.
The coach has given special meaning
in a sweetish haze every action bleak after bleak.
They don't grow back. Barren mind as armfuls of space.
Words of reclamation. A concerned word.
It was remarked that I the house spots.
Night spots or the house in French.
The playland a space of somnambulant ambient and thou.
There was a deep hillside cut of light
and invisibility. Places where the bed called out in the evening.
Trace forwards and backwards the forest in the tree.
Why those echoes suddenly appear everytime intimations
of an e c h o in the meaning forest.
The switch we do when birds every sleep and sing.
How much can paper in the headlamps.
Comment your country. A clear sun prey doing
well around a worker.
The tired daunted feeling from the product lying
and distinct from the dream job beginning.
Adjoining said ditch. How heavy shapes dream metal pigs.

# Incognito Exploded Alphabetically

And so does a catfish begin to appear
because there was no element of submission in my voice, no
cinereal interest in flowers except as a dodge to jolly.
Discontinued style a two-bar, dark-field beveled velvet,
flared arms, slacks off, curio suspension, roiling biceps
available in almond, furnishing sharp sights in darkness,
entertainment touch and go, pass the solitaire.
Digitally reversible into eternity bibliotherapy bio-as-say
fluctuant accident prone plot's worth of pianos,
every grand,
every professional upright,
every player,
every digital,
every concealed hood,
every previously owned waterfall seat,
every inner spring and contemporary shadow,
absolutely cineangiocardiographic hero-blasted.
Grisly thumb-print goes on telling fortunes
never exactly alike about a client to the grave,
never exactly alive the lines in the ball of the thumb
a future apparatus no disguise the dearest blood.
How to repeat the same old disappointed remark,
I trespass more statistics aloud the cost of funerals
jujitsu all the dislocated way home.
Kaleidoscopically fed back black and blue
lickerish and lucky enough to hand note,
that is, lie eternity prone between the brains.
Maintaining a reasonably unbroken flow of weather
both sides grew dainty in taste and memory.
Not obligate but roll arms, break mania together.
One night—it was towards the close of the war.
Presently presently panoramic a long glance
quark part of the city repeatedly the whole
stranger here itself always near.
Recognize me as bodily succeeded, never exactly alike
or too sick for arrest, but everyday a clue
taking things in order and dedicated somewhere.
Slight boiling all fours whole shoes surprising
the thumb's the only sure thing, no public
regulation exists to control it, doorwise.

Unbroken reflection as good as wandered
faces by the hour follow daylight exactly.

from *Civil Noir*

As matter: of particles I may as well come down
without another word (the dream a cinema deprived
of public, cordial mitral valved lying and being
you-ed atonement, she's too sliced for landing
to rare flowered bookie arms to can't talk now
her hands are dropping big lug spora to it was more
than Friday to o' the people with a black ball of fire
inside and outside a head maintaining the rhythm rhythm
of trade trade official culture soak to simultaneously
projected toughness and warmth, cynicism and sensitivity
and as for using eyes the incidental winking and blinking
animal watch me read seeing this the tone will glint
raunchy magnificence) but first please attention please
bring the demo room up to the front desk back up to this
fresh early place

DEAR TEACHING USING EYES:
GOOD TO SAY IF YOU CAN GET IT BUT NEVER PINT AT
WATERMILLIONS WHEN JOBS VANISH WHEN BLINDS JACK
SHUFFLING SLIDING OR TAPPED IN UNCONSCIOUS
IMITATION THEM CHORDS GRABBED JUST LIKE THAT
this nod to bougainvillea lit slantindicular playing
fork in the road backed up years to this day: airish.

MEANT AWHILE THE SAME SMALL TIME:
institutional augurates
power strapped little towness intestimony to thought
(towels for instance) prosaic with psychic gore,
patriotic fizz ed distress bed; re-input Ozzy Osbourne
about a million in the afternoon...

bye-bye love cocoa phenomenal
mighty recreation privilege
nightymightymighty calamity halo
nightymightymightymighty baroque love

(at the feet of teen preacho on the hillside
miraculous military pictograph coincidentally
scorned cells, portraits of the criminally familiar
in a naturalist frenzy of expectant sails,
clouds, foam, land, cold spit on raft
the flesh swept theme of disaster
one saliva bubble of spatial hysteria tinguished...
let me tell you about this place:

Text-ray emission: graveyard weather scene
from old fruit jar information and how
they keep secret house from so & so
                              Out to Here
...by the day...by the week...if this is a house...
the land it is on in a fency country sends no & no
letter but ploos of bare bones furniture lingual
creek counting "C-r-e-a-t-i-o-n!" thought I
better to tell a stranger (my peers, however,
are you made of?) CLIME UPSET TALL TELLING
read with difficulty the bored page is rage
spread thin as before and after *there*
the fustest with the mostest chattel indebted
plant mind hazard inauguration here ye's.

Onto molecular rivets cleansed fingertips out of the heat in a high strained valley, even thought white gloves a place out on paranoir this summer. Should somebody see sober hand shouts of light shot ragged blotto here-ville moving blobs very somebody seen history. Confidential and sweeping anything on me abstract hard lower lip genre neglect without children sudsy transition for the brief flashing record into mind squads smile a praise. Sentimental all toesy spells come of age starring an American. Latter day body intrigue thick beastly TV control beauties even. No I's on the blind side of houses watch the street after awhile frantic things shake loose hearty muttered guest of mouth I'll watch the house while you drink it hit a wall before we saw it. A series of the world smithy tire sing, fog smell, kelp rot, just try it shadows first noticed by French in the mirror with deep, distant eyes. The tearing sound tore it slowly time after time with her teeth the handkerchief came to tear it out and bit on it. As if to peer eyes open flick decanting the shine of them practically nothing visible even in darkness.

"Not if they sniffed him, miss."

Haw grave drawl something blinked line on the wealthy well grand a crack, everything on the red. Dictation dedication to and from inter (negative) memory indigo so Stanwyck fans out white earth. Enter (time) law of the golf course bravos grill breech drill melt socketry furious y más con stuck thunko, clubbed treeless aim, ate heroic steak, nice sore us genre, fat rink fingers running. Dear stranger or a rock to dilate upon. Blossom is bazoom swell hiddenness, born with "veils" over faces, etc. Toothy rattled eye more than accuracy I hear numbers flashing, smacked wave pseudo-dancing under the pretty strong blue dress, chéri. Coincident idea tefloned to pay hell alley iron word skillet helicopter leavings. Justifying mental cuts 'n scratches, it went everywhere, divided bandage debacle between loss and memory. Irreparable the incapacity? Now or then miraged much later symbolic barrier with a secret plan, virtually ocean with no one in charge.

"Simulated glory glory stain."

Scalded by the faith of ink a charging elk and lost it. Favorable but of course inconclusive private efforts a habit, combat, a canard portmanteau. A chair you should have brought with you here. Blandly personnel file the book, icebox, all. The article sounds bright instantaneous structural patter inside job gravitational. (Fig. 1. hat more or less meant.) Gabbled menu, meet hypergorge. Magneto-pause, the conky summer league. Notes on autobiographically reversed rear window plots: rumpled spectacles, broke shirt, smirking head falsie, shoe squirts, cold poke throws its voice bricks. Room filling chemistry ultra-ultra *this* in public: for want of a better habit, conjecture a handkerchief slowly dried the face continuing here. She just got a glass of water from the page. Part what goes over a fence last.

"The very ground hard as flint."

# Jessica Grim

## Vernal Pyrexia

Their world hurts

the silvery commute
asks all the wrong questions

resilient flirtatious *word dough*

non-returnable
my face becomes liquid, we bottle it
inside its numbness a brain begins to work again
the flag is crawling on the street .
our excess pacifies us

specimanship recant
ego trudge wakes
spring's lewd pairings
duplicate seasonal
stones on my breath

fevers eat my soul
divestiture propeller
weighted forward from its trunk

finally its death throes stop moving hysterically
even where enemies become the wind
without leggage
sips

almost continually stepped on
it's our pleasure

neck size predicts
shoots from the hip
totally clavicle
bound up
youth flutes

pull sound from meaning
along its side
now
soldered
sight relapse
glittering film of sand

interviews fall like wire brushes

traceries lash
straight out of the imagination

descriptive function
sounds which emit from the ear
like ripples in a lake

colossal mediocrity hounds
we shine our purse to make
sure the money has a nice home
each with different posture
aromas
the insides bubbling out as it roasts

a glance at the knee
splayed

it agitates until
murky past engorged
so much plastic attack
thimbles tumble out
turns in at the ankles

prosody's hit parade

unit penance
they lack the ballast

inevitable tremors

looks at her with those squid eyes
we want it raw
surface surface your skin politics
languor

abutted sky crane
dystopic enzyme eats thought
pocking it with little groans
so sweet, so salty
what candor to expose the message like that
I vote for portable desks,
breast pumps

it just wouldn't *stretch* over that much flesh
agit prop
preparatory plug
experience the taste

coterie
subatomic
preamble to deluge
provides your sinewy joy
arbitrarily indifferenced

I'm too too retrograde, so?

*bargain* with your influence
freeway delirium ducks out of my shoes just in time
tinseled memories ached to show us their clammy smile
seeps within earshot

gurney has laid
out on it the aluminum residence of my soul
severe overreaction of water to fire
wants an easy hanging truth

magnetic *sepia* attack
leggy turned soil touts anti-germination soliloquy
abused battery holders

uncut prism balloons out into the sea of rage
it tattles on itself

it seemed more possible
desire sewn into a pocket
erupts tenderly

in order to inflate the sense of self they
annihilate the utopian concept of "you"

geography of soul *cartouche*
typifies hostile equation

the work of signification powers its way to doom
leitmotif reincarnates itself
in full view of her breast

drenched camouflage adheres like a skin
sex of starvation
it's already investigated
tragic asters bloom
your eyelids tell the truth

the orifice of the law
stampede
we see *our* window reflected in *their* window

certain words marked as slogans
pull the surface down

bold stake through the heart
why so cagey?
misogynistic tendencies under bisexual gloss
no time like your life span
shot down with *and* by

shocked building falls into the street
peaceable rubble
they urgently grew another head

neo neo audience-seeking talent

they felt their brain rescuing them
augers ill

sarcophagal
molting pheasants can barely fly
autumn is the season of dispersal

planetary consciousness pervert
twiddles the globe

you're a known carcinogen
strategist finally exhales
*on me*
glyphic cassettes sinew past reader heads
archly capacitative, capillary
render butter

low cross excites

bring back sisters
bring back carriage minutes
when you go it looks positive
lugs away
his hand flapping
afraid of leakage

everlasting immediate future
leg attacks the pure hand growing younger
slippery-eyed cloth on midriff
swabs the earth

in the calibrated heat they suck
situational hardballs

there's no problem because we swallowed it
their loges
retractable truck spins out
flirt box

I lost track of how painless it was
their mother on a stick
stands up
under its tactical profile
the ground rushes up
in the wilderness of chance

renditions eat you

the breaking economy can't make it better

# Untitled

Moving the memory back out to accommodate its fixation, its thickness. Dried sprig of jasmine... alternating between a readiness to be deceived by my own fantasies, and then remarkable daylight breaks in.

In my thinking where...could this be you indeed.

Really a very detailed description of some skin, is that a prelude?

Vestige-less again! Special abilities, in some vast way, two-fold cowardice. Linkage sever unfelt. We have counted as high as we can go, held our breath that long. Geographic punctuality, worries are seasonal, and heady. No time out.

That peculiar void waving at the end of your rope, "make it real." Whose words follow: flagtime stops. Research melodious possibilities. Infolded spectaculars. My specious mind. Funny how we gravitate. Positioning sharply into the fetid dusk. Scant starry field throws off a furlong scent.

Rich with it. Tallness a metaphor, the down slant. Comeback with motives on your shirtsleeve, sexy litigious gratuities. Skate free of the hole once it's carved. Through it darkness and indiscretion. Successive meanderings, veneration of ego. I would like a control-top sort of gig. Rangy synthetics clasping my breasts. Fully fragile carpathian.

Venal arteries. Her clear heart. The muscular anticipation. Because the supposed perception (the record, the death) forefronts *her* difficulties with that stance. Cutting bruising wounded flesh as the body of the writer, what now.

Also in an iron surface. The vanishing striptease inside the glass throne. Brittle green algae. Neck curves to hold the light. Only barrenness will make you calm... that flat arena whereby exquisite sameness proceeds. Murmur vibrates as our tongues touch at last.

In the destroyed view of the world a room. Empty and level both. A genius lust, the skins of things walk past.

# Untitled

pull the plug on the self

limitations arrive outside all view of them
understand it as literal
too caustic

her inerts

that you get constructed *inside* the language

oedipal misconcepts     throwing off light     frames hum
        obviating it
vestal soap
solitarily committed

knowledge of you exists and
so much so

propositions' tumbling

that pillowy moment where possibility starts
        has small range

living example of euthanasia fails
the vessel
        substandard quiver
completely boldly accept
an organ stops
privatized tier

needfully attendant
the inner life
        (you like it here?)

eventually we rescue it
        cloud cover, oracular covets

(our arms straddle the shape as if feeling
        the shelf beneath our feet)

      they shade it in
tandem succulence
emptiness locates, then lodges

contiguous pleasures arc out
          monitoring, estimable

fasten on this as its own desertion

thin thread predicated within the mechanism

hope, too, spectates

# Diminishment Falls

I.

Flitting around the solid buttes
softly weightlessness
the description by itself full of holes
a word for every design

masking galls
heavy aroma of predation
each step an agony of sympathetic charm

it happens to you because the facade and the inner workings
don't match

grottos lounge on coast
locate the viewfinder, then dazzle it
arbitration bondage

dysfunctional alphabet
your horizon comes to meet you
on the inside and the outside of a building

fog touches the crenelated bone of grief

disk swings on its outer axis

what your dream awakens in you is terror
hobbled by its many faces

inside the heliographic edge emergent foam
day after day it begins to find you

slow sound stigmatizes
intimate need to stay surface
tourniquet thrills, house of prose, topiary gaze
swimming under a wide flat hull
the nameless longing breaks down
delicate blue interior

II.

The facile it
surrounded
metallurgically

prehensile, pieced worth
cagey escapism
utilitarianism readjusts
then went to meet him

comprehensive paucity
aerates the form

no ploughs
legacy like a rock

she came to the man as if he were gold, leagues away
the way they rig it plunders
believe the city when it needs you

she seemed disconcerted
just watch

shell of hope
they looked so fragile in coming to our side
it shows up in the pinkish sick-looking dusk
as emotions

you bag it



III.

Has to do the life anyway

groupings slow down
margin of error at this point
diminishing

our convex vocabulary is finished once and for all
though some complexity did touch the surface
I can almost taste it
cut off at the wrists

body alone inherits tension
spectral framework focuses out
active urban decoration

my eyes sought the plinths

# Peter Ganick

## 4 "starts" from AGORAPHOBIA

### I

commonsense worn awash
in a fertility as correct as
with a score secondary to
perhaps the jabber toss,
at vertical introspection on
contours evoke
a lack of purposelessness,
in a world thought imperils
light by inattendance,
already eyes shift
to entice generative intervention
in particular the danger of remorse,
toil at what's possible to toss
becomes in focus to remove &
to restore potency for angles
of disagreement,
the packet regroups
what overviews lacked,
before uncertainty as abstraction
that often carries
whose intention is as if variable,
someday resurrects as instance
for spooled noises,
the candid entry,
a patriarchy secure on tangents
to the riddle
befriends each & every
whose baggage expects delivery
& the feat that arrives
endured by a piracy too close
or too far,
all return for a closeup,
inner tension
adjudicates forms to click,
looks forward & reasons about

with which kept at this house calls:
concept-restructuring,
toned louder than ambition
experience pronounces delivery
of a rumor conducted
from a surprise,

tetherball soon as restrictive as
intractable compares an intersection
of automatism to the
infancy of a dimmed belle
whose roller coaster has no plan,
juxtaposed in poem
is a cluttered response,
how brought to conceit fulfills
all warned & instantaneous drivers,
certain toxins redirect
whose ending in a route commences
in choice of all that could make
frequently & competently
a rumor to
disguise selection,
any more they'll be unspecified
as newer than
a ring of telephone drama,
there's a hesitancy of qualifiers if
the reduction materializes &
sends away from the majority
of candor,
the shot-put as regulative
as anyone can be by *semper fidelis*,
insist upon a site cracked for queasy
informations
left uptown in ajar,
before the quintessence of
squalor beyond whitened opera,
parchment in fifteen minds
intervenes through regulation as
car-horn sediments invite captives,
one can always run up credit
& be open,
a wall manages tempests

that engrave on stray minds,
their inert aspects
not more than ten are filled
to gather conduct
in stable exemption,
gone schoolward to a

## II

Where is silence magnified by a contortionist on
the stereo? to befriend a space becomes trivial for
cling frequencies of tended demand.

Are shared spaces the elephant of insouciant build-
up cornered by an *oeuvre* of discrete tempi? can
deep darling's putty-glazed eyes ask for a firmness
mostly independent? brought in from months of
precision where does the inescapable readjustment
close in even further?

Do these court alignment against or for anyone's
details of crude ingenues result in felicitous
sandstorms? was the triatholon not avarice? is it
also safe to talk reason to what was once urgent? is
becoming a role of time passing the corrected
savior of a melody no one expects?

Why talk with those people before memory sets in?
why negotiate elegant somethings any car seat
could often rehearse for during the wet-season
weekend?

Think: what if arrays develop a yellow cape? how
deep will assignments need restructuring on a full
basis for punishment? does each arrangement
survive? can nature get by the gorge insolent as it
matters to the greatest clone to differ up until now?

Could one sleep here by the dream unanswerable
to the pharaoh passed by by centuries? urgent
options culminate in an expression whose pressure
demands adjustments and refines others to capably

fixate on whomever the legal monotony assumes
would be bitten; are the days of silence between calm
stereophonic surpluses, one ear on the bias,
self congratulatory at best?

Do other pariahs (if severed from tighter
etiologies) mask paradise windows with certain
sleepy drought? the forceful water escapes once
and for all in a germane trajectory to paradise.

Something to think about: expansivity (where
earlier there was a model for all those who went by
moods imperiled and not to fight about): would it
kick what is ready to bail out on shore-leave?

Waters imply no salutation for a chorus of angels
reduced by non-proliferation agencies, does inward
forgetting allow this?

Who reacts against a pale divider's track-record?
on floods of looking back through waiting-game
salutations; are you ready to talk about personhood
amidst letting go from the curious demands? one
betting-shop wore plateaus before the mind of
sitting correctly.

Are doings the reasonable curiosity of faked
silence before ignorance? as development becomes
fractional, to embrace with sorrow the freedoms
ascertained as previous is it likely nothing will be
done before capitulated servants? whose pirouettes
deny a book rather light into carousels? a tempo of
well-wishers, all blind (in and out of focus) for
material binaries that contort precedent, stunts of
mental and physical silence combine well with
creative enlistment of dual purpose.

Does pleasure as a career's pronouncement that
breathes easier during procedural overruns
become materials' puzzle?

## III

Jarred from its clotted thimble and new to the
challenge, given no chaired escape, one's reductive
gambit closes as the mauve island retains
enticement with echoes; plus, it is agreeable to
slow-dance the fruit of a tricked dander, any
partisan entropy can begin reassurances; brain-
dead from overt lyric appeal, candy oceans whose
familiar dedication happens no more without
caffeine assaults gets round to a fearful distance;
calls off a clipboard surface in procedural attitudes
drop-kick the blood-red title, an apple pause is
devoted to tapper; bitten through that moment
called independence, a ritual precedent of font
camera dances (almost fused) are pitted against a
damask telethon, obtuse as presence wanes the
lock, affably recued to the meteor before begun or
blackened.

Had they patted the patience of noon
barring being boastful,
each grievous symmetry would call for music
however
the last person attaches no results
to its impatience;
the story leaps, this virtuoso there
and by the knife
whose edge of curtailed amnesia sits in silence,
the practice of everyone floods a wide river
a usable ocean, though there are no thanks
whose tools crave sediment, each thousand is
limited to being
weary or blunt.

Never refuse nectar from the aggrandizement of
code; twixt worlds that assume favor, no warning
that a girl's comet has flourishes of adulation; this
is the region tapestries rope down, this is the
futures' binary difference.

A tactical slaughter-house on the periphery of a
cackling voice, the true guardian binges on receipts
always to relax his scepter in driest twins; treacle
calls for a sham act of simulated beginnings, each
datum is soon weeded thrown and presented at a
time often attended and above all correct, fully
materialized by whatever the flaxen widget retains
of a community of intelligence, every yardsale
inches toward supervision; write a word and that
becomes texture, asphalt heard aghast though
timed to grapple with the instructor,
could noble vastness of purpose could refer only to
time-space, silence is the black matter of a resin
that collects on sadhus' feet.

Think of tone as
place, result, and echo;
of time as an ingredient essential to music already
predicated by thickly-saturated egalitarianisms;
waves and curiosity are there about now.

Science and linguistics invade letters' highest
residue, thought is a dodge twixt hunger in space;
no one wiser act happens anymore; a certitude
whose neon revisionary tactic picks up nettles on
its shoe, the formless anonymity walks streets in
factual effort.

Those sent on impact resign for now because a
siphon was glued to rescind all light; through song
and rhythm each cluster of attribute is not
dissonant or forgotten;
far targets in a forum on aetheric dynamos, outside
the count of practicality reads *voiced as beauty,
tentative and superficial,* haggard time changes in

## IV

As a target for She,
the obvious icon.

At a month's slide
She always talked something
over in the environment,
how the She-label indicts
vacant memory.

She: infertile of time,
here aware insistently
that removes concrete
idioms.

    (ditto carouse on
    that operate)

Where instances of
She attracts marbled earth,
the stand of implication
is His.

She, the His of once
active choice,
replay Her identifies:
target,
a least tiny earth no stereotype
of His that She activates
for Him.

    (one's corridor
    skirts destitute entries
    on happened form)

So that He becomes, She
is act of will,
terrified of His aptitude

such that Her icon walks through
a storm around the huddle

A dirted sky-romeo, His
article refers
ahead to tyranny, goes a
day at a time, callous
for Her the
embryo determinant to
begin topic.

      (set to literature,
      so that
      no one thought)

      (that will
      resonate,
      a foreigner taps
      in front)

Dry as a contrast,
a telephone form, She, the
spotted leg of
His identity, spared in
oppressive anarchy.

Still, the experience She invites
to beget is
traffic of His vanity,
the matter of all direct labels,
all Her/His behind
a collective motive.

No islands compare Her
to the motion
of His escape, or, talk
through little packages invasively
harder,
things to do.

# Louis Cabri

## Shooting pains the rifle said

| | |
|---|---:|
| Since that habitual | *bad* |
|     Maze! Looking itself | spoof on a toilet |
| Army | pile up |
|     Master | plan far- |
| Slung | machinic indifference temple |
|     Credentials counter | marble sweat |
| My head over the sink folks | if we're *that* |
|     Forklift | constructed bath with teeth |
| Destroyed every visible trace | quarkening back the beat |
|     Alligator lesson | lesions |
| Enzyme Of | foe, f |
|     Attack | bunting |
| He's been sickly | Crimea |
|     Mother | rivet |
| Plot to take over government | boxed |
|     (Father) Nefarious | dildo vectors |
| Deadheads, on the teenager's face | explode over |
|     Bubbles | the deep |
| Is precisely where there's problems the man said, but later denied the | medium |
|     October | blue |
| Report that "convicted the criminal," the man said but later denied that | media the fall |

| | |
|---|---:|
|     A cured sausage is<br>    a hardened sausage | har- |
| There was any mention in the report<br>however a setup allegation | -ness- |
|     Bert, or cousin Bret | -racy- |
| Is not | balk |
|     Collects | canvassing |
| A broomful | -to- |
|     Moping around the confectionery | will |
| But a fictive | sill occupied |
|     Slide- | force |
| Replay says | leech |
|     Fund | the room for |
| Sent shivers | governor |
|     Of a mucky roof | television |
| Painfully where minutes before I'd sat<br>with the generals, a diplomat<br>born to the station | rhino planet, like that |
|     Of principles | stat- |
| Given the lie, the evidence | cotton |
|     Exercising | twirlers |
| Slipped | half part |
|     Punt | bat- |
| Out of control, down the<br>banister when he was | *in anus* |
|     Magnanimous | mat- |
| Just a man, who's been<br>electrocuted | con fed ally, mum |
|     Singer, rancher, mechanical | |

                beast feeding patent-                              gums sal-

Add or take away from the essential being?
retorted the priest to reporters
gathered around the crippled                                       design

                Singular                                            frozen

In the wheelchair, while he pushed                              the fence

                Hair                                                  crop

His whole being, fed
fitfully to memories of                                          the stream

                Washing                                            laterally

Distractedly at her wristwatch to the
point of                                                              even

                Filter                                                sleep

Where just the music sufficed to calm her,
seated before speakers, the lights out                              pipe

                Blood                                                   in

God appears to a man in                                vectors to a species

                Crystal                                          vernacular

Blue jeans from ads when reducing quality                        grin, do

                I'm in time                                          spec-

Who cares, the workers?                                            tickles

                International brain wave                             half-

The government spokesperson said, in a                        fast blow-

                Gum                                              accountant

Ungartered                              swirl *yes*-colours outnumber!

                Pin                                                     up

Response like
a true homosexual, snorted the                                     diaper

Cabri/363

| | |
|---|---|
| Out | flak |
| Pained | contribution |
| Trooper | of the cereal box |
| Oppression nosedives | guaranteed |
| Para- | chute |
| On his face | a smile that said I dare you |
| Dental | work speaking freely! |
| Convinced that no fellow | Barbie |
| Convict The | will |
| Vegetable | jump, oil |
| Tray of | *fags* |
| Is being released into | glamour |
| Troy | parking lots |
| Bar counters | aside, |
| Through envy | spent on |
| Hugged the wall | criminal behaviour |
| With ants | exaggerated their involvement |
| In prison | when it happened |
| Skill | crust |
| Released, causing havoc in the neighbourhood where | rum & coke afternoons |
| Cruise | punishment |
| To rehabilitate convicted | social organ |
| Habitual maps | NEED NOT APPLY |
| Meant feeding them | race |

| | |
|---|---:|
| From the ground | up, toboggan Algonkian |
| Lanced boil, then proceeded to ask an | flavour |
| Equation | stranger |
| Escalating | mood machine |
| Said hospital | alien |
| Series of embarrassing | burn out |
| Boo | bacon end |
| Terminally ill patients | shy? |
| Boo | diorama |
| About your health plan, the good doctor said | unfortunately |
| Is dead | the squeeze |
| In protection of | your life away |
| Consoled | to basement consoles |
| The law | arrives |
| In packages of ten | complete in pink |
| Sells sneakers tomorrow at K-Mart | as a |
| Free | me |
| Really | |
| Digested | |
| When *you know and I know* a Totem | feeder |
| Sleep | chain |
| Shooting pains | pigeon parallel says rubber |
| Prefers | agreeable |
| Rifle Dip | late |

| | |
|---|---|
| Slouch | sounding |
| Encounter | arrives |
| To vanish meant | *the toggle switch* |
| Dispersal wound turn this in dispatch | comfort |
| A leaky | *to your neighbour* |
| Kettles a profligate beach | calm your Arnie bites |

# So how's the Dow

|  |  |
|---|---|
|  | I dunno, how's it with you |
| In the float-based market capitalization index | Sprung a leak |
| Of a public sphere | In your face |
| Where attention accrues share liquidity | There's condensation |
| It's best to use clear distinct strokes | On ideas |
| Of a little less than a second a piece | That fuck |
| And abhor disconnected details | That |
| Are accountable | To partitions |
| For as participants we're key informers | "    " |
| Though not all analysts attach importance to performance | – My wad |
| As an indicator of future profit levels |  |
| For temps and card stock holders | It's a mausoleum! |
| An indexical structure of brand relief | *The same* |
| Is the afforded mechanism of compensation | For four, please |
| Within dominant environments | Like me |
| While systematic thought under topics | Being |
| Keeps squalor out and freshness In subject variations | Sexed |

| | |
|---|---|
| The index constituency receives | A barmitzvah! |
| Barring war, riot and natural disaster | – A breakneck fate |
| Preferential rates | Skimmed off |
| Even as vital signs decrease | Aplomb |
| Recession-resistant pharmaceuticals add shine and control | Resumes |
| To a portfolio's asset composition | Résumé |
| Whose will only two decades ago | Thunder |
| Spoke within eight years of retirement | Like a charm |
| As the security and intelligence service | Lily pad |
| To its captive client base | |
| After in-house counselling | Floats |
| With public report updates | In high or low pressure zones of |
| That namby pamby crypto-communist left wing NDP anti-NAFTA alliance | |
| And other databases stand by | Retiary biostats |
| This plot of dials | A tingling in the fingers |
| The hoped-for licensed cop's incensed tactics of refusal | Figures pointing |
| Polished with grift | |
| From direct correlations of state-sponsored violence and public activism | To switch theorists |
| A Calvinist strain from the Tower of Babel | – Feebs |

| | |
|---|---|
| Tripling redemption fees in white and auxiliary heathen markets | Flush |
| Committed or permitted alignments in advance | To lust |
| As advertised traits | Mixer "on" |
| Hired for results of total return | Dusting the bongo drums |
| Merge cartels | Your "yes" vote |
| To manufacture incidental | Testtube baby |
| To providential | Protocol |
| Insurances against obligation | Fobs it off |
| For the shoes et cetera | As stack repair |
| Or ahnbahrah de shwah' of rules | Wears |
| A body | Gymnosoph |
| Out-fit by deontological chokepears | Chapter |
| Surmises in welfare rococo | The end of |
| Corporate memory's coping pins ado | "Fuck you" |
| To indebt every cognate object | Let's split this spleen |
| For interest-bearing account | Or mount |
| Of swingin' the consonantal emporium— | Or count |
| Glamor | A diptych |
| At the K-Mart of inscribing | A motto daub |

*for the* barscheit *index*

# The Practice of Art

## Ron Silliman

It should be writ large, for all to see: **we in North America are living in a poetic renaissance unparalleled in our history.** The riches of this book make the case. That this should be so is worth noting as well as worth asking why and what it means.

The premise of this book is quite simple — that there is so much good poetry and prose of a formally progressive impulse now being written beyond what was anthologized in Douglas Messerli's *Language Poetries* and my own *In the American Tree* that another gathering is warranted. The reality far exceeds the claim: the questions that will haunt Dennis Barone and Peter Ganick, just as they have bedeviled me and every other individual foolish enough to attempt such a collection, will ultimately be one of boundaries. Why this writer and not that?

That's an impossible question under the best of circumstances, which is why all anthologies must fail. That question also insists that the circumstances themselves need to be interrogated. In *The Art of Practice*, a single act has pushed this book toward a specific and somewhat unusual shape. *Practice* has been deliberately organized around a blindspot — any writer who appeared in either my anthology or Messerli's was not considered. However, it's essential to recognize what this book is not: *In the American Tree: The Out-takes* or *Language Poetries: The Next Generation*[1]. Neither of these two earlier books ever set out to represent the big picture of what we might think of as Post-New American Poetry. In doing so, Barone and Ganick have had to confront a vast amount of interesting, intelligent, often breathtaking and groundbreaking writing. And what they have come up with — just like what I and Messerli came up with — can be read best, I believe, as a series of pointers rather than as an inclusive or complete thought.

My own response to the problem of too much good writing from which to choose was to focus on a hopefully well-defined, but consciously narrow solution. Only those writers whose work had appeared repeatedly in a specific set of public venues were considered. Good writers whose work appeared only a few times in these settings or whose writing never appeared in them at all were left out. But this still left me with far too many wonderful poets to ever imaginably include, so, with a heavy heart and more than a little guilt, I left out those poets whose work had already achieved a separate and distinct public identity prior to the emergence of language poetry in the early 1970s, who took a public stance that seemed skeptical if not openly critical of language poetry, as such, or who wrote from within national contexts other than that of the United States. Although this process meant that I could not include some people whose poetry I believed to be among the very best and most important being written (Steve McCaffery, Tom Raworth, Beverly Dahlen, Norman Fischer, and Ted Pearson, for example), my method had the advantage of leaving me with relatively few "borderline" cases over which to agonize. And I absolutely managed to blow some of those, such as the omission of Abigail Child on the grounds that she was then better known as a film-maker. My method also had the side-effect of giving the *Tree* an air of militancy that was (and still is) misleading. I consoled myself with the knowledge that this "militancy" — vague echo of the heroic stage of Surrealism — caused the book to become much more widely read than otherwise would have been the case, especially once critics like Tom Clark and Stephen Schwartz volunteered their own personal public relations campaign on its behalf.

In this sense, *The Art of Practice* stands as a rebuke of my own method — a valuable and necessary correction. (And no doubt of Messerli's as well, who had much more serious page limitations to contend with than I had to face.[2]) But the result is that this collection actively intends itself to be read alongside these two earlier anthologies. And that is the level at which its larger coherence comes most sharply into view.[3]

As a survey of the broader horizon of the progressive tradition in North American poetry, *Practice* offers roads into many of its most significant dynamics. Two appear on the first page in the work of Susan Clark, a Canadian woman. Women outnumber men in *The Art of Practice* — quite unlike *Tree* and *Poetries* — not out of any editorial sense of redress, but because margin and center have shifted over the past decade. Many of the women whose work is collected here began to publish widely only after 1980 *and/or* can be read as much as a critique by example of a narrowly configured (and macho) language poetry as they can be read as a part of it.

Of particular importance has been the journal *HOW(ever)*, whose editors included Kathleen Fraser and Susan Gevirtz, with assistance from Dodie Bellamy, Rachel Blau DuPlessis and others. *HOW(ever)* functioned much like *This*, *L=A=N=G=U=A=G=E*, and *Roof* five to ten years earlier to define and bring together a community of possibility for writing. The depth of its impact can be felt throughout this book. That other women also have stepped into controlling the processes of production, both as editor and publisher (Susan Clark, Melanie Neilson, Jessica Grim, Dodie Bellamy and Leslie Scalapino are all examples), can at least in part be traced back to this newsletter.

Like U.S. poetry, Canadian verse has been undergoing a renaissance that dates back 30 years. Canadian poetics initially snuck across the border in the writing of David Bromige over two decades ago, but, beginning with Steve McCaffery, the late bp Nichol, collective writing projects like The Four Horsemen and the Toronto Research Group, Coach House Press and the Kootenay School of Writing, it has increasingly become one of the driving forces changing the way Americans as well as Canadians write. *Practice* notes this by both beginning and ending with "northern" authors[4], with four others in between. Canadian poetry is both like and unlike that of the U.S. "Your monsters are our monsters," Colin Browne once said to me of our relative literary traditions. And yet that's not entirely true. One cannot imagine contemporary Canadian poetry without the impact of its own modernism, especially the work of Louis Dudek, whose poetry (deliberately distanced from the modernism of Williams, Stein, and Zukofsky) has been neglected in the U.S. The invasion of the San Francisco Renaissance that began with the Vancouver Poetry Conference of 1963 and the later migration northward of Robin Blaser, Stan Persky and George Stanley did give Canada a strong dose of U.S. influence, but one largely free of the boring academic strains that make so much Yankee verse a suburban snoozy affair. Nor can one imagine Canadian poetry without acknowledging the impact of francophone poets, starting with Nicole Brossard[5] – a phenomenon that has no exact equivalent in the US[6] – and through francophone poetry to the literary and intellectual traditions of France. Although it's not particularly visible in this volume's selection, the French influence on a Canadian poet such as Steve McCaffery has a different context and meaning to it than the French influence on Craig Watson, Norma Cole or Mei-Mei Berssenbrugge[7].

Both the Canadian presence and the French flavoring in *Practice* point to the increased transnationalism of the poetry scene over the past decade. While many of the direct and indirect ancestors of these authors urged an international reading list and often translated work of great interest and value into English, the emphasis previously focused for the most part on texts of the canonized dead. Now, however, some hint of the long-rumored global village is beginning to come true in poetics. Vancouver's Jeff Derksen can give a reading to an interested audience in the Canary Islands and one can speak of the influence of Leslie Scalapino on post-Soviet Russian verse. And they likewise will prove knowledgeable about the writing of their own generation in such far away places.

Of course, influence travels across time as well as space. *Practice's* passionate relationship to the New American Poetry of the 1950s and '60s may be more visible than that of the *Tree* only because of the lower level of militancy in editorial focus. Fraser, who might have appeared in the original Allen anthology had not Robert Duncan pushed its editor away from a New York School focus more toward Projectivism and the San Francisco Renaissance, represents the most direct link. Beverly Dahlen's relationship to the Spicer Circle of the 1960s — deliberately outside the phenomenon, outspokenly critical of it, and simultaneously in a dialog with it so intense as to make her poetry one of its most important products — has been very nearly duplicated by her relationship to the more recent generation of language poets. Norman Fischer writes a poetry that simply abolishes formal distinctions between these two generations of verse. Fischer's work, in fact, offers the quintessential evidence for the argument that language poetry (so-called) embodies a direct extension of the New Americans, albeit an extension that transforms and problematizes its own understanding of what came before. (Would Duncan recognize his own influence in the works of Aaron Shurin here, or Frank O'Hara his impact on the role of the line in Elaine Equi's texts?)

A second thread of influence connects these poets to Objectivism, the tendency that directly preceded the New Americans but whose impact, for reasons of history, occurred only well after the generation of the Allen anthology was going full bore. In fact, John Taggart and Rachel Blau DuPlessis can take a good deal of credit for having brought public attention to the writing of Louis Zukofsky and George Oppen, respectively. Perhaps because of this late reception, the range of influence of these two Objectivists has been so vast that the close reader can spot it here in the exactingly wrought stanzas of surf poet Stephen Ratcliffe and in the way found materials become simultaneously lurid and opaque — *Catullus* meets *Capital* — in Joan Retallack's *Errata 5uite*. The "typo" in Retallack's title is a quintessentially Zukofskian effect.

Other notable tendencies that run through *Practice* include the partially overlapping categories of New Narrative and post-identity-politics gay poetics (Dodie Bellamy, Aaron Shurin), the interdisciplinary aspects of the New York arts scene (Abigail Child, Johanna Drucker, Fiona Templeton), and the rigorous and cognitive aspects of surrealism (Jerry Estrin, Jeff Derksen, and Norma Cole most visibly, but present not far beneath the surface in maybe another dozen contributors). In each instance, a long and historically specific process well worth exploring further can be found. What these impulses share, beyond the broadest strains of reading and influence, is a renegotiation of center and margin in which the concept of centricity itself is challenged or denied.

Virtually all of the poets here have been influenced by – and have influenced – the poets collected in *Tree* and *Poetries*. From my (admittedly biased) perspective, the most profound aspect of this influence has been that work which, like Beverly Dahlen's or Jerry Estrin's or Leslie Scalapino's, can be read in part as a deep critique of the assumptions (and presumptiveness) of language poetry. Because of Barone and Ganick's decision to exclude all poets involved in the earlier collections – including Nick Piombino, whose theoretical writing was included in the *Tree* and who didn't fully emerge as a poet until the mid-1980s – this critical response to language poetry becomes an unspoken unifying principle of *Practice*, connecting such diverse writers as Gil Ott, Dodie Bellamy, Hank Lazer, Jessica Grim, Dennis Barone and Spencer Selby. But what is not to be found here is a single critique or line[8]. Nor, for any one of these writers, is that critique primary to their own literary project. Instead, each poet, by example, demonstrates possibilities for verse *beyond* that which you will find in the two other collections.

This demonstration of method gives the lie to what might be the easiest possible misreading of *The Art of Practice* – that, because this collection lacks a selection of the critical writing that distinguished the *Tree*, these poets are themselves any less "theoretical" in their concerns or practice than the writers from the other two books. Many have written theory, given talks, and been actively involved with the editorial and critical functions of poetry for years, often with great impact. Indeed, several of the first poet's talks that gave language poetry its sense of cohesion and purpose took place in Abigail Child's Folsom Street loft in San Francisco in the late '70s. Like Steve McCaffery's transformation of poststructuralist theory into practical strategies for writing, Dahlen's recuperation of Freud into feminism has shown this theoretical streak to be fearless, as has Scalapino's insistence that any possible history of the avant-garde include perspectives outside the Eurocentric confines of its origins. At least half the poets here have served as editors of journals or books, or coordinated reading series, taking direct responsibility for shaping the poetry community in which they participate. But, as always, the test of theory must be the writing itself. Thus, while John Taggart's unpublished doctoral dissertation on the work of Louis Zukofsky remains one of the two critical texts all Zukofsky scholars must confront, Taggart as poet has extended the Zukofskian commitment to the primacy of the signifier into the ecstatic functions of song, a use that *"A"-1*'s depiction of Bach's Saint Matthew's Passion could never have imagined and one that Taggart seems to set quite consciously against the more secular music of a Clark Coolidge, not to mention the sound poetry of a McCaffery.

If the critical dimension of poetry remains as thick and intense here as in *Poetries* and *Tree*, one difference that should be noted is geographic. With the sole exceptions of Tom Beckett, a health inspector in Kent, Ohio, and Clark Coolidge in the Berkshires, the 40 poets gathered in the *Tree* came from a handful of metropolitan areas: the San Francisco Bay Area, New York City, San Diego, Washington, and Boston. *Tree* represents a poetry of urban literary scenes, continuing a process that had been staked out for an American avant-garde long before the Allen anthology (where the itinerant Projectivists were the closest thing to an exception, although even they were characterized as the Black Mountain school[9]) – the progressive tradition in poetry (as in so many other arts) has been an explicitly urban phenomenon, against which, for instance, the McPoem of the Iowa Writer's Workshop has represented an historically (and politically) suburban response[10]. *The Art of Practice* demonstrates a diaspora, although by no means a complete one. In addition to poets from Canada, we have writers from Alabama and Arizona, Philadelphia, Chicago, New Mexico, Ohio, Connecticut, and Shippensburg, PA. I'm not certain what exactly to make of the fact that the six writers who all have strong current or recent connections to New York City – Child, Drucker, Grim, Neilson, Equi, and Templeton – include no men, but I do note that five also have strong connections with other geographic writing communities. On the other hand, sixteen of the 45 poets here have participated actively in the poetry scene of the San Francisco region, and at least two others, Hank Lazer and Gil Ott, lived in the Bay Area earlier in their lives. Clearly, to whatever degree postmodern American poetry has a center, it is one that has moved west and is rapidly spreading out.

Barone and Ganick might have edited *Practice* so as to emphasize this geographic shift, or the critical dimension of the poetry, or its relation to any number of other things. But books have limits, none more painful than those of anthologies. For every poet included here, two others had to be left out. I don't agree with the final list of inclusions and I doubt that any single contributor to *Practice* would either. We each have our own definitions of what matters most and our reading lists are driven by such passions. While I would obviously recommend that anyone who enjoys *The Art of Practice* seek out the poets included in *Language Poetries* and *In the American Tree*, I would even more strongly urge this same reader to seek out the work of the following writers: Kathy Acker, Charles Alexander, Michael Amnasan, Michael Anderson, Dawn Michelle Baude, Scott Bentley, Julia Blumenreich, Bruce Boone, Nicole Brossard, D.F. Brown, Lee Ann Brown, Gerald Burns, Lisa Cooper, Bill Corbett, Lydia Davis, Christopher Dewdney, Steve Dickison, Barbara Einzig, George Evans, Steve Farmer, Phillip Foss, Ben Friedlander, Ed Friedman, Gene Frumkin, Forrest Gander, David C.D. Gansz, Amy Gerstler, Michael Gizzi, Peter Gizzi, Robert Glück, John Godfrey, Janet Gray, Bob Harrison, Leland Hickman, John High, Crag Hill, Andrea Hollaway, Robert Hunter, Kenneth Irby, Margaret Johnson, Ronald Johnson, Beth Baruch Joselow, Lawrence Kearney, August Keinzhaler, Kevin Killian, Wayne Kline, Ann Lauterbach, Karen Lessing, Joel Lewis, Lori Lubetski, Bill Luoma, Nate Mackey, Tyrus Miller, Harryette Mullen, Kofi Natambu, Gale Nelson, A.L. Nielsen, bp Nichol, Maureen Owen, Ted Pearson, Dennis Phillips, Ray Ragosta, Dan Raphael, Jed Rasula, Pat Reed, Phyllis Rosenzweig, Joe Ross, Jerome Sala, Andrew Schelling, David Shapiro, Gail Sher, Gerry Shikatani, John Shoptaw, Joseph Simas, Pat Smith, Rod Smith, Susan Nash Smith, Juliana Spahr, Gustof Sobin, Cole Swenson, The Theory Girls, Steve Tills, John Tritica, Lorenzo Thomas, Chris Tysh, George Tysh, Fred Wah, Keith Waldrop, Rosmarie Waldrop, C.D. Wright, John Yau, Geoff Young, and Karl Young. These writers, who outnumber those included in the *Tree* and *Practice* combined, are doing important, exciting work that, if collected into this format, would yield a gathering equal to the trio of anthologies produced to date. That more than 160 North American poets are actively and usefully involved in the avant-garde tradition of writing is in itself a stunning thought. That this is the one literary tradition to value rigor and the personal responsibility of the author for all aspects of the work only underscores my original assertion: **we in North America are living in a poetic renaissance unparalleled in our history.** And I've neglected to mention writers from Britain, Australia, France, Italy, Spain, China, Japan, Germany, and the former Communist nations who are themselves adding to the conversation. Although this may come as a surprise to those whose exposure to verse has been limited to the pre- and anti-modernist worldview of America's establishmentarian institutions, we live in a great time for poetry. Read every word.

# Footnotes

1. This certainly is not a collection of "the next generation." At least three of the writers here, John Taggart, Beverly Dahlen, and Kathleen Fraser, were not considered for *In the American Tree* because they had already established themselves as mature poets in the 1960s before any of the publications around which my anthology was organized came into existence. I went to college with Aaron Shurin and Stephen Ratcliffe. And some of those whose work has only become widely available since the editing of the *Tree* and *Poetries,* such as Margy Sloan, Spencer Selby, the late Jerry Estrin, Laura Moriarty, Peter Ganick, Norma Cole, and Hank Lazer, are all over 40. Including poets who began to publish later is one of the ways in which *Practice* does a better job of representing a broad and loosely defined generation than the earlier books. Of the 45 poets here, perhaps half did not begin to publish widely until after 1980.

2. I "solved" my own problem of space when Carroll F. Terrell accepted *In the American Tree* sight unseen after the original publisher, Ross-Erickson, dropped out. Terrell felt honor-bound to go forward with the 600-page book in spite of its economically disastrous consequences. Even though it's the National Poetry Foundation's best-selling volume, *Tree* will not begin to break even until a third printing has sold out. *Tree* is now in a second printing.

3. This no doubt is the rationale for asking me to write the afterword. One significant caveat here, however, is that *In the American Tree* was edited during 1981-2 and *Language Poetries* a year or two later, so that the trio of books does not exactly stand as a cross-section of a literary community in time, but rather in motion, a target that's perpetually reinventing itself.

4. Followed, in the first instance, by one of the editors, and preceded in the last instance by the other editor, just to gently underscore the point that this sequence is by no means accidental.

5. Limiting the *Tree* to US residents tugged at my own anti-nationalist impulses. But I could not imagine including Canadian poets in the *Tree* without using Brossard. Which not only meant having to figure why I should stop at Canada when I could include some great British poets like Tom Raworth, but also why not bring in such French poets as Claude Royet-Journaud or Anne Marie Albiach. Ultimately, to my mind, crossing one border led to a logic of crossing them all and there aren't that many aesthetic steps from Clark Coolidge to the Siberian-born Ivan Zhdanov. A book that

incorporated the progressive tradition in poetry as it now operates internationally may not be a do-able project, but would be a truly amazing collection.

6. That there isn't (yet) a Spanish-language equivalent to the formally progressive, internationalist tradition in the US is disturbing. In addition to the generations of economic and cultural repression that Hispanic Americans have suffered, it needs to be remembered that Spanish culture in the US is not a "European" tradition — which the internationalist avant-garde community largely may be — and that, even if the language does offer an indirect pathway back to that tradition, that, *after World War 2*, Spain of all NATO countries did the most to destroy its own incipient postmodernism. Only now do we see poets such as Estaban Pujals, Carmen Africa Vidal and Manuel Brito making attempts to jump start a moribund literary tradition.

7. The difficulty one has pinning down the specifics of influence and nation are well demonstrated here. McCaffery, like David Bromige, was born and spent his youth in Great Britain. Cole has spent time in both France and Canada. Berssenbrugge's life has gone from China to New Mexico and her interest in new French poetry seems to have developed away from the Burning Deck-New College-*O·blek* projects that have been its major routes into the US poetry scene. In much the same way, of course, the question of Canada must always be one of *which Canada*? With an East-West geographic span equivalent to the US and a population roughly equivalent to that of California, Canadian poets have a very different set of relations between individual, community, and nation to negotiate.

8. Not that language poetry has ever presented a single point of view on anything, including how to say and spell its name. Robert Grenier's "On Speech" and Ted Greenwald's "Spoken" in the critical section of *Tree* demonstrate the absolutely contradictory stances that have been taken.

9. A site where some never once set foot.

10. One might argue, following that line of reasoning, that the future of an avant-garde tradition in the arts depends very much on the political health and future of the cities. And to some degree this is true, but only once we recognize the meaning of a book such as *Practice*, which might be said to reflect an urbanization of the suburbs and internationalization of secondary urban centers.

# Selected Bibliographical Information

Todd Baron. *Return of the World* (O Books, 1989); *(this . . . seasonal journal) (. . .)* (Paradigm, 1992).

Dennis Barone. *The House of Land* (Spectacular Diseases, 1986); *Forms/Froms* (Potes and Poets, 1988); *Waves of Ice, Waves of Rumor* (Zasterle, 1993).

Dodie Bellamy. *Feminine Hijinx* (Hanuman Books, 1990); *Answer* (Leave Books, 1992).

Martine Bellen. *Places People Dare Note Enter* (Potes and Poets, 1991).

Mei-Mei Berssenbrugge. *The Heat Bird* (Burning Deck, 1986); *Empathy* (Station Hill, 1988); *Sphericity* (Kelsey Street, 1993).

John Byrum. *Cells* (Abacus, Potes and Poets, 1988); *rImage* (Tsunami Editions, 1990); *INTERALIA/among other things* (Leave Books, 1992).

Louis Cabri. Poems in *Writing* 27 and *Motel* 5.

Susan Clark. *Believing in the World: a reference work* (Tsunami Editions, 1989).

Abigail Child. *Climate/Plus* (Coincidence, 1986); *A Motive for Mayhem* (Potes and Poets, 1989); *MOB* (O Books, 1993).

Norma Cole. *Mace Hill Remap* (Moving Letters, 1988); *Metamorphopsia* (Potes and Poets, 1988); *My Bird Book* (Littoral, 1991).

Beverly Dahlen. *A Reading (11-17)* (Potes and Poets, 1989); A *Reading (8-10)* (Chax, 1992).

Daniel Davidson. *Product* (e.g., 1991); *Image* (Zasterle, 1992); *Weather* (Score, 1992).

Jeff Derksen. *Down Time* (Talon Books, 1990); *Selfish: Something Deep Inside Liberal Cultural Relativism Says "Yes I Can"* (pomflit, 1993); *Dwell* (Talon Books, 1993).

Johanna Drucker. *The Word Made Flesh* (Druckwerk, 1989); *Simulant Portrait* (Druckwerk/Pyramid Atlantic, 1991); *OTHERSPACE: Martin Ty/opography*, in collaboration with Brad Freeman (Nexus, 1993).

Rachel Blau DuPlessis. *Gypsy/Moth* (Coincidence, 1984); *Tabula Rosa* (Potes and Poets, 1987); *Drafts (3-14)* (Potes and Poets, 1991).

Elaine Equi. *Surface Tension* (Coffee House, 1989); *Views Without Rooms* (Hanuman, 1989); *Decoy* (The Figures, 1993).

Jerry Estrin. *Cold Heaven* (Zasterle, 1990); *Motion Speaking* (Chance, 1993).

Norman Fischer. *The Devices* (Potes and Poets, 1987); *Turn Left in Order to Go Right* (O Books, 1989); *Precisely the Point Being Made* (O Books/Chax, 1993).

Steven Forth. *Calls This* (Abacus, Potes and Poets, 1987); *Imitating Flight* (Tels, 1986).

Kathleen Fraser. *Each Next* (The Figures, 1980). *Notes Preceding Trust* (Lapis, 1987; *When New Time Folds Up* (Chax, 1993).

William Fuller. *byt* (O Books, 1989); *The Sugar Borders* (O Books, 1993); *The Central Reader* (Paradigm, 1993).

Peter Ganick. *Remove A Concept: parts 1 & 2* (Leech, 1990); *News on Skis* (Avenue B, 1992); *Agoraphobia* (Drogue, 1993).

Susan Gevirtz. *Domino: point of entry* (Leave Books, 1992); *Linen Minus* (Avenue B, 1992); *Taken Place* (Street Editions, 1993).

Jessica Grim. *Intrepid Hearts* (Coincidence, 1986); *The Inveterate Life* (O Books, 1990).

Hank Lazer. *INTER(IR)RUPTIONS* (Generator, 1992); *Doublespace Poems, 1971-1989 (Segue Books, 1992)*.

Andrew Levy. *Values Chauffeur You* (O Books, 1990); *Democracy Assemblages (Innerer Klang, 1990); Curve* (O Books, 1993).

Colleen Lookingbill. *Incognita* (SINK, 1992).

Karen Mac Cormack. *Straw Cupid* (Nightwood Editions, 1987); *Quill Driver (Nightwood Editions, 1989); Quirks & Quillets* (Chax, 1991).

Steve McCaffery. *Evoba: The Investigations* (Coach House, 1987); *The Black Debt* (Nightwood Editions, 1989); *Theory of Sediment* (Talonbooks, 1991).

Douglas Messerli. *River to Rivet: A Poetic Trilogy* (Sun and Moon, 1984); *Maxims from My Mother's Milk/Hymn to Him: A Dialogue* (Sun and Moon, 1989); *Silence All Round Marked: An Historical Play in Hysteria Writ* (Sun and Moon, 1991).

Laura Moriarty. *like roads* (Kelsey Street, 1989); *Rondeaux* (Roof Books, 1990); *L'Archiviste* (Zasterle, 1991).

Sheila E. Murphy. *With House Silence* (Stride, 1987); *Sad Isn't the Color of the Dream* (Stride, 1991); *Teth* (Chax, 1991).

Melanie Neilson. *Prop and Guide* (The Figures, 1991); *Civil Noir* (Roof Books, 1991).

Jena Osman. *Twelve Parts of Her* (Burning Deck, 1989); *Underwater Dive: version one* (Paradigm, 1990); *Amblyopia* (Avenue B, 1993).

Gil Ott. *within range* (Burning Deck, 1986); *The Yellow Floor* (Sun and Moon, 1987); *Public Domain* (Potes and Poets, 1989).

Stephen Ratcliffe. *[where late the sweet] BIRDS SANG* (O Books, 1989); *spaces in the light said to be where one/comes from* (Potes and Poets, 1992); *Selected Letters* (Zasterle, 1992).

Joan Retallack. *Circumstantial Evidence* (S.O.S./Edge Books, 1985); *ERRATA 5UITE* (Edge Books, 1993); *How To Do Things With Words* (Sun and Moon, 1994).

Leslie Scalapino. *way* (North Point, 1988); *How Phenomena Appear to Unfold* (Potes and Poets, 1989); *Crowd and not evening or light* (O Books, 1992).

Spencer Selby. *Instar* (SINK, 1989); *Barricade* (Paradigm, 1990); *House of Before* (Potes and Poets, 1991).

Aaron Shurin. *A's Dream* (O Books, 1989); *Narrativity* (Sun and Moon, 1990); *Into Distances* (Sun and Moon, 1993).

Ron Silliman. *Manifest* (Zasterle, 1990); *Demo to Ink* (Chax, 1992); *Toner* (Potes and Poets, 1992).

Margy Sloan. *Infiltrations* (Queriendo, 1989); *On Method* (Abacus, Potes and Poets, 1992); *The Said Lands, Islands and Premises (Chax, 1993)*.

John Taggart. *Loop* (Sun and Moon, 1991); *Aeschylus/Fragments* (Parallel Editions, 1993); *Standing Wave* (Lost Roads, 1993).

Fiona Templeton. *London* (Sun and Moon, 1984); *You—The City* (Roof Books, 1990).

Craig Watson. *After Calculus* (Burning Deck, 1988); *Unsuspended Animation* (Paradigm, 1990); *Picture of the Picture of the Image in the Glass* (O Books, 1992).

Eric Wirth. Remarks on writing in *O.ARS* 8 and 9 and *Aerial* 6/7.


These publications are available from Small Press Distribution, 1814 San Pablo Ave., Berkeley, CA 94702 and in England from Paul Green, Spectacular Diseases, 83(b) London Road, Peterborough, Cambs., PE2 9BS.

Potes & Poets Press, Inc.
181 Edgemont Avenue
Elmwood, CT 06110

## POTES AND POETS PRESS PUBLICATIONS

Mickal And, Book 7, *Samsara Congeries*
Bruce Andrews, *Excommunicate*
Bruce Andrews, *Executive Summary*
Bruce Andrews, from *Shut Up*
Rae Armantrout, from *Made to Seem*
Todd Baron, *dark as a hat*
Dennis Barone, *The World / The Possibility*
Dennis Barone, *Forms / Froms*
Dennis Barone, *The Book of Discoveries*
Lee Bartlett, *Red Scare*
Beau Beausoleil, *in case / this way two things fall*
Martine Bellen, *Places People Dare Not Enter*
Steve Benson, *Reverse Order*
Steve Benson, *Two Works Based on Performance*
Brita Bergland, *form is bidden*
Charles Bernstein, *Amblyopia*
Charles Bernstein, *Conversation with Henry Hills*
Julia Blumenreich, *Parallelism*
David Bromige, *Romantic Traceries*
Paul Buck, *No Title*
Gerald Burns, *Seventeen Poems*
John Byrum, *Cells*
O. Cadiot / C. Bernstein, *Red, Green & Black*
Abigail Child, *A Motive for Mayhem*
A. Clarke / R. Sheppard, eds., *Floating Capital*
Norman Cole, *Metamorphopsia*
Clark Coolidge, *The Symphony*
Cid Corman, *Essay on Poetry*
Cid Corman, *Root Song*
Beverly Dahlen, *A Reading (11-17)*
Tina Darragh, *a(gain)2st the odds*
Tina Darragh, *Exposed Faces*
Alan Davies, *a an av es*
Alan Davies, *Mnemonotechnics*
Alan Davies, *Riot Now*
Jean Day, *The I and the You*
Jean Day, from *No Springs Trail*
Ray DiPalma, *The Jukebox of Memnon*
Ray DiPalma, *New Poems*
Ray DiPalma, *14 Poems from Metropolitan Corridor*
Rachel Blau DuPlessis, *Drafts #8 and #9*
Rachel Blau DuPlessis, *Drafts 3-14*
Rachel Blau DuPlessis, *Tabula Rosa*
Johanna Drucker, from *Bookscape*
Theodore Enslin, *Case Book*
Theodore Enslin, *Meditations on Varied Grounds*
Theodore Enslin, *September's Bonfire*
Elaine Equi, from *Decoy*
Norman Fischer, from *Success*
Norman Fischer, *The Devices*
Steven Forth, *Calls This*
Kathleen Fraser, *Giotto : Arena*
Peter Ganick, *Met Honest Stanzas*
Peter Ganick, *Rectangular Morning Poem*
Peter Ganick, *Two Space Six*
Susan Gevirtz, *Korean and Milkhouse*
Robert Grenier, *What I Believe*
Jessica Grim, *It / Ohio*
Jefferson Hansen, *Three Poems*
Carla Harryman, *Vice*

Carla Harryman, *The Words*
Susan Howe, *Federalist 10*
Janet Hunter, *in the absence of alphabets*
P. Inman, *backbite*
P. Inman, *Think of One*
P. Inman, *waver*
Andrew Levy, *Reading Places, Reading Times*
Andrew Levy, from *salvage device plants*
Steve MacCaffery, from *Theory of Sediment*
Jackson Mac Low, *Prose & Verse from the Early 80's*
Jackson Mac Low, *Twenties (8-25)*
Barbara Moraff, *Learning to Move*
Laura Moriarty, *the goddess*
Sheila E. Murphy, *Literal Ponds*
Susan Smith Nash, *Scenes from Hollywood Babylon*
Melanie Neilson, *Civil Noir*
Janette Orr, *The Balcony of Escape*
Jena Osman, *Ellerby's Observatory*
Gil Ott, *Public Domain*
Maureen Owen, *Imaginary Income*
Maureen Owen, *Untapped Maps*
Rochelle Owens, from *Luca*
Bob Perelman, *Two Poems*
Nick Piombino, from *The Frozen Witness*
Larry Price, *Work in Progress*
Keith Rahmings, *Printouts*
Dan Raphael, *The Matter What Is*
Dan Raphael, *Oops Gotta Go*
Dan Raphael, *Zone du Jour*
Stephen Ratcliffe, *Sonnets*
Stephen Ratcliffe, *spaces in the light said to be
    where one/ comes from*
Joan Retallack, *Western Civ Cont'd*
Maria Richard, *Secondary Image / Whisper Omega*
Susan Roberts, *cherries in the afternoon*
Susan Roberts, *dab / a calling in*
Kit Robinson, *The Champagne of Concrete*
Kit Robinson, *Up early*
Leslie Scalapino, *clarinet part I heard*
Leslie Scalapino, *How Phenomena Appear to Unfold*
Laurie Schneider, *Pieces of Two*
Spencer Selby, *Accident Potential*
Spencer Selby, *House of Before*
Gail Sher, *w/*
James Sherry, *Lazy Sonnets*
Ron Silliman, *B A R T*
Ron Silliman, *Lit*
Ron Silliman, from *Paradise*
Ron Silliman, *Toner*
Margy Sloan, from *On Method*
Pete Spence, *Almanak*
Pete Spence, *Elaborate at the Outline*
Thomas Taylor, *The One, The Same, and The Other, 7-9*
Liz Waldner, *The Way You May*
Diane Ward, *Being Another / Locating in the World*
Diane Ward, *Crossing*
Craig Watson, *The Asks*
Craig Watson, *Drum*
Barret Watten, from *Two Recent Works*
Hannah Weiner, *Nijole's House*
Matt Wellick, *Imperial Mind*